HANNA R. SANDVIG

INSTAGRAM

FOR

Fiction

Authors

HOW TO FIND READERS, BUILD COMMUNITY, & *Sell* MORE BOOKS

INSTAGRAM

FOR

Fiction
Authors

CONTENTS

Introduction..9

How to use this book...13

Interview: Hanna Sandvig......................................15

PART 1: THE BASICS

Chapter 1: Setting up your profile........................23

Interview: Alana Albertson.....................................27

Chapter 2: The time investment...........................31

Interview: Heather Kelley.......................................37

Chapter 3: Bookstagram vs Author Accounts.......43

Interview: Kim Chance...51

Chapter 4: Creating a cohesive feed....................57

Interview: Caroline George....................................63

Chapter 5: Photography...69

Interview: Sarah Moore..77

Chapter 6: Selfies...81

Interview: Kealan Patrick Burke............................85

Chapter 7: Planning your posts.............................91

Interview C.E. Clayton...97

Chapter 8: Hashtags...107

Interview: Harriet Young.......................................113

Chapter 9: Following hastags................................119

Interview: Danielle Jensen................................123

PART 2: CONNECTING WITH READERS

Chapter 10: Engagement................................131

Interview: Samantha................................139

Chapter 11: Measuring and tracking engagement........143

Interview: James Fahy................................149

Chapter 12: Selling books................................157

Interview: Becky Moynihan................................161

Chapter 13: Building Community................................167

Interview: C.M. Karys................................171

Chapter 14: Photo challenges................................177

Interview: Kandi Stiener................................181

Chapter 15: Increasing Engagement................................185

Interview: Kay L Moody................................191

Chapter 16: Gaining Followers................................197

PART 3: BEYOND THE BASICS

Chapter 17: Stories................................205

Interview: Tyffany Hackett................................209

Chapter 18: Ideas for stories................................215

Interview: Faroukh Naseem................................221

Chapter 19: Live................................225

Interview: Briana Morgan................................227

Chapter 20: IGTV...231

Interview: Valia Lind...235

Chapter 21: Reels...239

Interview: J.M. Buckler.......................................241

PART 4: INFLUENCERS AND BOOK TOURS

Chapter 22: Influencers.......................................249

Interview: Audrey Grey.......................................255

Chapter 23: Bookstagram tours...........................261

Interview: Storygram Tours................................267

Chapter 24: Representing other businesses.........271

Interview: Christine Manzari..............................275

Chapter 25: Book boxes......................................283

Interview: Fae Crate..287

Interview: Nerdy Book Box.................................291

Chapter 26: Working with artists on Instagram....295

Interview: Arz28..299

FINAL THOUGHTS

Troubleshooting..304

Conclusion...306

Resources..308

Accounts Interviewed..312

Glossary...314

Acknowledgements..317

INTRODUCTION

Hi! My name is Hanna, and I love Instagram.

Back in 2017, eighteen months before I published my first book, I had an art Instagram account that was getting very little traction. I had just started writing a draft that I was sure would be the book I'd finally finish and publish (I was right). Then a friend started a bookstagram account, and when I learned what that was, my mind was blown.

There was this whole community of people who just took pretty photos (I love pretty photos!) of books (I love books!). These were readers who read as much as I did, something I rarely come across in real life, and in the same genres as me. I had found my people.

I took that art account and started posting photos of books—books I read, books I illustrated covers for— and my account grew, slowly but surely. I started with about a hundred followers, and by the time I published my debut novel, I had broken a thousand. That's small potatoes in Instagram terms, but I was thrilled. This was an audience of one thousand people who loved books like mine. A thousand people who cared, at least in passing, about what I wrote, drew, and read.

Just by posting occasionally about my upcoming book and directing people to the link in my Instagram bio, I gathered a hundred people for my newsletter. Again, that's not millions, but I didn't even have a book out yet. That was a hundred people who found the idea of my book interesting enough that they didn't want to miss its launch.

I put together a cover reveal tour with help from the friends I had made during that time and put up a pre-order. My launch sold about fifty books. Okay, so I didn't make millions on one book, and I'm not going to pretend that you will either. But that book continues to plug along, giving me steady sales and page reads every month for a year and a half now.

And my following is growing, collecting momentum for my next launch.

I'm not an outlier. I didn't make a bestseller list with my first book. But I gathered friends and fans on Instagram and gave my career a great start. And if I can do it, you can do it, too.

However, I know my advice is just that: mine. There are authors further along in their careers than me who are absolutely killing it on Instagram. Why don't they write a book about it? Too busy being awesome, I guess. I'm constantly trying to learn more about Instagram, so I decided to interview them and see if we could both learn how to level up our Instagram accounts and sell more books.

So, in addition to my own findings, this book also contains advice from the best authors (both indie and traditionally published), influencers, and book tour companies I could badger into answering my questions. I learned so much from them, and I hope you will, too.

For every Instagrammer I've interviewed, I mention if they are a bookstagram-style account or an author account, which I'll explain in more detail in Chapter 3. I also include their follower count at the time of publishing this book and their account handle. Follower count isn't everything, but I think it's still an interesting bit of data to compare. I really recommend looking up the accounts on Instagram as you read. Instagram is a visual platform, and you'll learn so much more from seeing how successful accounts look and checking out how they engage with their followers. There's a master list of all the accounts interviewed both in the back of the book and at www.instagramforfictionauthors.com.

You might notice that some of the advice given in interviews varies from mine. I actually love this, because it shows that there are many ways to use Instagram, depending on your personality and the genres you write in. I've tried to be well rounded in my advice, but of course I'm still biased, and you need to figure out what works best for you.

HOW TO USE THIS BOOK

There's a lot of information in this little book. Read it through, take some notes, and decide on one or two things to try. Then, in a month or so, try a couple more. Don't try everything at once! Or at all. To implement everything in this book, you'd have to stop sleeping or cut down on your writing, and those are both terrible ideas.

I'm not trying to tell you what you must do to succeed. I hope that reading this book will inspire you to try new things, to make connections and build relationships. To be creative visually, not just with words. Instagram can be a lot of fun. Don't be afraid to dive in and experiment.

You may notice that I haven't included any information on boosted posts or Instagram ads. This is simply because I've yet to meet an author who's been able to use them effectively. I hope this changes in the future, and if it does, I'll certainly update this book!

Because the Instagram app is always changing and updating, I'm not focusing as much on how to use the app from a technical standpoint. In the six months I've been drafting this book, they've moved Live videos around three times, introduced Reels, and changed the algorithm. I don't want to update this book every time a button changes, and a book really isn't the best format for showing you how to handle the technical side.

Instead, this book will focus on the principles and strategies that will help you grow an audience and engage readers, no matter what little things change on the app itself.

On to the first interview! I thought I'd start at the beginning. With myself.

INTERVIEW WITH: *Hanna Sandvig*

Handle: @hannasandvig
Followers: 3k
Account style: Bookstagram (author)
Genre: YA Fairytale Retellings

How long have you been on Instagram, and where were you in your publishing journey when you started?
Three years. I started a year and a half before publishing my first book.

What's a mistake you see authors making on Instagram?
Combining their personal and author accounts. It's better to split them into two accounts. If all I see is your baby /horse/lunches/hikes, then how will I learn anything about your awesome books?

Which posts get the most engagement for you?

My own cover reveals. Other than that, it's mostly dependent on my caption and how much people want to respond to it.

What's your favorite thing about the community?

I love the bookstagram community because none of my real-life friends are as obsessed with books and writing as I am. Bookstagram is a place where I can geek out, and use that geekiness to showcase and hopefully sell my books.

Do you have a strategy for balancing the sort of posts you make?

I'm a bit overly particular about balancing my feed. I alternate between four photo layouts, and make sure to share my own work at least 1/3 of the time. I post a selfie every fourth photo. And I try to balance my favorite popular traditionally published books in my genre (to gain more attention) with indie books that I love or am promoting for my friends.

What do you take your photos with? Do you use any editing software?

I take my photos with my Canon 6D, edit in Lightroom on my desktop, and doodle on the photos with Procreate. I also use Photoshop when I need to add text or mock-up a book cover.

What are a couple of caption types or questions that you like best?

I love asking people about themselves. What they're reading or watching. What their favorite dessert is. It's fun to hear from them, and people love to talk about themselves!

How personal do you get on your account?

I do use my real name, and I occasionally show my children (but I don't give their names). I keep it light and happy on my main feed. My Stories are a bit more unfiltered, but I still try to focus on aspects of my life that my followers will be interested in. My books are a fun escape from reality, and I want my Instagram account to feel similar.

How much time do you devote to Instagram in a day or week?

I spend probably an hour or two a day, split up. I once had an app that tracked it and then I told that app to mind its own business. For the images I use, I spend an hour or two a week taking and editing photos. And I often have Instagram's direct messages open on my computer because it's one of the places where I talk to my friends.

INTRODUCTION

PART 1: *The Basics*

Chapter 1: SETTING UP YOUR PROFILE

If you aren't already signed up for Instagram, I hope I've convinced you to give it a shot. If you are signed up, you might still pick up a few tips from this section. Let's go over the basics of setting up your profile.

Account Type: First off, obviously your account needs to be public so that people can find you, and I do think that you should get a professional account, not a personal one. I've heard some chatter about Instagram suppressing professional accounts the way Facebook suppressed pages, but I haven't had that experience. They seem to mess with everyone equally.

The main thing that changed when I switched to a professional account was that I got access to more data. More on that later. You have a choice between Business and Creator accounts. Choose Creator for more nuanced data on your audience and a more flexible inbox. Choose Business if you want to be able to schedule posts through a program like Hootsuite. You can always switch account types later.

Profile Photo: I recommend an actual photo of you. It helps build relationships if people know what you look like. Unless you have a super-secret pen name. It's also nice to use the same profile photo across multiple platforms and not change it super often. This makes it easier for people who are searching for you to know that they found you and not someone else with the same name as you.

Name: Use the name you publish under.

Username: Use the name you publish under and add "author" at the beginning or end, unless you have a good reason not to. My account is 50% about my books and 50% about my art, so I still just go with my name.

Website: You can only have one link here, so send them to buy your books. But what about your newsletter, and your merch shop, and your really cool Facebook group?

There is a workaround. Make the link open a page with more links. You can set up a page on your website to send them to, or you can use a service like Linktree or url.bio. That's what I do.

You can't have links in your posts at all, and you can't add links to your Stories until you have ten thousand followers, so it's very handy to be able to tell people that the link is in your profile and have more than one link there. But that does mean that people have to click an extra time, so it's a trade-off.

Bio: Make it snappy, and only include the things that your ideal reader cares about, such as "Author of books about crime-solving kittens." You can add a second sentence but they will have to click to read it, and they probably won't.

Story Highlights: Anything you post in Stories disappears in 24 hours. But, you can immortalize especially lovely Stories in Highlights. Highlights are groups of Stories that show up on your profile. We'll get into this more in Part 3.

Okay, you're all set up! Now you just need to add some posts.

INTERVIEW WITH: *Alana Albertson*

Handle: @authoralanaalbertson
Followers: 25.8k
Account style: Author
Genre: Contemporary Romance

How long have you been on Instagram, and where were you in your publishing journey when you started?
I joined Instagram in January 2017. I already had many bestsellers by then (a book that hit #3 on amazon, multiple top 100 books) but I was releasing less due to health problems.

Do you feel that Instagram helps you sell books? How else is it helpful to you as an author?

Yes, absolutely. It is also a great way to connect with my fans.

Do you do anything special for a book launch on Instagram?

Yes, I create a complete launch strategy for each book. Stories, a feed grid, countdown posts, and Instagram ads.

What's a mistake you see authors making on Instagram?

Not planning what they post. Normally I plan my posts out 60 days in advance.

Which posts get the most engagement for you?

Gorgeous pictures of my cover models, my pets, and pictures of me.

Do you have a strategy for balancing the sort of posts you make?

Yes. For years I hated posting pictures of myself. So now I try to balance book pictures with pictures about me/slice of life.

What do you take your photos with? Do you use any editing software?

My photos are professionally done. I also occasionally use stock and The Image Apothecary. I edit in Photoshop Elements.

Do you take your photos in batches, or do you take them and post them immediately?

Batches. I never post immediately. All content is preplanned.

How personal do you get on your account?

Not that personal. I do show some pictures of my family.

Do you have any other tips for authors on using Instagram?

If you think your readers aren't on Instagram, you are wrong. Instagram is essential for authors. Make a plan to grow your following.

Alana Albertson has a great course for authors on using Instagram at:
www.authoralanaalbertson.com

Chapter 2: THE TIME INVESTMENT

Okay, okay, Hanna," you might be saying. "I hear you. But how much time is this Instagram nonsense going to take?"

You're busy. I understand. I have three children, two in school and one still at home during the day, and I'm an author and a freelance illustrator. The other day, I bought a bottle of dry shampoo and then applied it two minutes later at the library while my kids were at craft club. Because I didn't have time to wash my hair that morning (too much information?). Life is crazy, and you don't want one more thing to do.

So, let's work this through. First, do you even need to be on Instagram? Well, that depends on what genre you write and who your audience is. There are a billion users on Instagram, and it's the social media platform used most widely by people 18-35 worldwide. So if your audience is mainly over 40, you may decide to spend your time on Facebook instead, but if you want that younger demographic, Instagram is your spot.

There's also a large community of readers on Instagram called bookstagram. Bookstagram is made up of mostly women aged 20-40. If you write fantasy, romance, or any genre of young adult fiction, bookstagram is a built-in audience for your books. I talk about bookstagram a lot in this book because even if you don't choose to create that style of account, it's important to be aware of the community and interact with it.

If you write books in other genres, you can certainly build a following on Instagram, especially if it's a platform you enjoy, but it might not be as large a part of your marketing plan.

Once you've decided to focus on Instagram, it can be helpful to think about how much time you want to devote to it. I've interviewed people who spend as little as an hour a week on Instagram, and those who spend up to six hours a day. More time, if spent strategically, will get you faster results, but most of us don't have six hours a day to devote to it.

Let's come up with three imaginary authors, with different amounts of time to commit, and give them each a strategy to match.

Author #1: 30 minutes a week

Let's call author #1 Dave. Dave is a successful thriller author and he doesn't have a lot of spare time, but he'd like to have a presence on Instagram. He's not planning to gain a ton of new readers, but he'd like to have somewhere his fans can find him, and a place to send people if he hires a company to do an Instagram book tour. He's willing to do a bit of work to get organized but then only wants to spend a half hour a week on Instagram.

1. Dave has some cash, so he decides to hire a local photographer to take some photos of him with his books and in his writing space. He also gets photos of his books with props that match his genre, and a few photos with an empty space where he can later insert a 3D mock-up up his upcoming new releases. Dave gets about thirty photos in all. If you have more time/photography skills than Dave, you can certainly do this

yourself, but there's no law that says you have to take your own Instagram photos. In fact, I'm interviewing a photographer who does bookstagram style shoots at the end of this section.

2. Next, Dave collects some quotes from his books and some excerpts from great reviews and hires someone from Fiverr to create thirty simple graphics that go well with his photos. As before, you could do this yourself, but Dave wants to save time for writing.

3. Dave posts nine images to start off his account, so that it doesn't look too empty, and then he posts an image once a week. He alternates between the photos and the graphics, and he follows my advice in the following chapters about captions and hashtags. He checks in at the end of the day and responds to all his comments.

Author #2: Two-three hours a week

Meet Vivian. She's a contemporary romance author. She thinks Instagram is fun, knows she has fans there and wants to grow her audience.

1. Once a month, Vivian does a little photoshoot and takes photos of her new releases and some of her favorite reads. If she travels somewhere pretty, she'll bring a book along and take some selfies while reading on vacation.

2. Vivian posts every other day, and is careful to respond to comments.

3. She posts a couple times a week in Stories with a writing update, or fun things from her daily life. She also shares any posts from her readers featuring her books in her Stories.

4. Vivian spends a few minutes a day going through her feed and leaving comments on the posts of readers and other writers in her genre to build community.

Author #3: One-two hours a day

Let me introduce you to Hanna. Oh, wait. That's me. Here's my Instagram routine.

1. Hanna takes photos once a week for an hour or two. Just one style of photos at a time, but she mixes them up in her feed to keep it balanced.

2. Every day, Hanna spends fifteen minutes going through her engagement groups (see Chapter 15) and liking all the posts, so she doesn't get behind.

3. She posts a photo six days a week. She responds to every comment on her photos and tries to go to each commenter's account to leave a comment on one of their photos.

4. Hanna posts in Stories daily, with at least one video post a week.

5. She spends a few minutes each day going through her feed and liking and commenting on her friends' posts as well as watching Stories (because she honestly enjoys Instagram).

Obviously, these are just examples. There are lots of ways you can spend your time on Instagram, but I hope that gives you an idea of some strategies to consider as you read the rest of the book and come up with your plan for having fun while growing your Instagram account.

INTERVIEW WITH: *Heather Kelley*

Handle: @read.write.coffee

Followers: 13.3k

Account style: Bookstagram (influencer & aspiring author)

When did you start your account?

About four years ago, I think. But I started scrolling back through my feed to find out for sure, and then decided I didn't have time for that and gave up. Sorry!! #TooLazy

Which posts get the most engagement for you?

Wouldn't I like to know?!! LOL. I check all the time to try and figure out a pattern, but it's unpredictable. The closest thing I've seen to a consistent rule is that pics of one of my daughters holding a book in front of my bookshelf almost always do well. Pics with one of my pets usually get a fair amount of engagement, too.

What's your favorite thing about the community?

I love having a space to gush about books with fellow bibliophiles. No one else in my real life (other than my daughters) read very much, and certainly not any of the same books as me. Here, I can pretty much always find a friend or two who has read my most recent book obsession.

And I love that it's given me the chance to meet a handful of people who I've really connected with and discovered that they are 100% MY PEOPLE and we chat all the time, and it means so much knowing I have them there whenever I need to talk about anything, whether it's how happy I am that it's raining or how bummed I am that I'm feeling stuck on the novel I'm writing.

What do you take your photos with? Do you use any editing software?

I have a nice camera (a Canon 6d mark II) that I use for all the pics I post to my feed. I edit mostly in Lightroom but sometimes a bit in Photoshop as well.

Do you take your photos in batches, or do you take them and post them immediately?
Oh, definitely in batches. I start to feel anxious if I don't have at least a week's worth of pics ready to go, lol. I like to take a whole handful of pics all in one spot, like on my bed one day, and then another day I'll take a bunch at my windowsill, and so on. Then I use the Later app to space them out so they'll look nice on my feed.

What are a couple of caption types or questions that you like best?
I love to do a fun predictive text caption but ONLY if I'm asking people to type out a max of four words before they start letting their phone fill in the rest. I get really annoyed when people want me to type "Once I went to my closet to pick out something to wear and I chose _____."

I also like to ask people what they've been loving lately, and share a few of the things that have made me smile, because it's uplifting to think about and write, and I always enjoy seeing everyone's answers.

Do you have any advice for authors on how to approach influencers?

Hmm, honestly, I would just say don't be afraid to ask, as long as you're polite and clear about what you're asking for (oh, and ideally follow the influencer before you message them). Right now, I have a lot on my plate and almost always have to turn down requests. But I would only ever be annoyed at being asked if someone was demanding or rude.

One time recently, an author asked if I could feature her book in my feed and I didn't have time, but she offered to send me a postcard and small goodie and I was happy to share those on my story, so being flexible about ways someone can help spread the word for you is great, when possible.

One last thing I would add is, if an author has taken the time to engage with me for a while and get to know me a bit—so that I would consider them an acquaintance rather than a stranger—I'm a lot more likely to try to make time for them even when I'm busy.

Do you have any tips for authors in creating a cohesive theme?

To me, it's easiest to create a theme around a simple color scheme. For example, my summer theme was mostly white with some pink in every picture. And keep your lighting as close to the same as you can all the time (randomly having some pics bright and others dark can break a theme). Then find an editing style or filter you like and use it for every single pic.

Also, when you're starting out with trying to keep a cohesive theme, it's a good idea to go really simple for a while. I'd recommend choosing two or three spots you like to use and doing very basic setups with your main item, a few carefully selected props, and plenty of white space. As a bonus, those shots don't take as long to set up as more complicated ones.

You're a photographer for Cherry Pie Author Services. How do you help authors with their Instagram accounts? I'm so glad you asked! I'm loving this new photography endeavor. It's a great creative outlet for me, and only occasionally a way to procrastinate writing my own novel. There are a handful of different ways that I can help writers who need a boost promoting their books or upping their social media presence.

One of the most direct ways is through the Book Promo Package where I take customized, beautiful pics of an author's book for use on their website, social media, etc. I also have a handful of pre-done sets of bookstagram pictures that can be purchased pretty inexpensively, for anyone who wants to start or improve their social media presence but doesn't have the time and energy to worry about it themselves. They're in themed sets and can be easily customized by adding a filter.

I also offer a package where I take custom bookish pics in whatever style someone wants, so if an author has an orange and blue book cover and wants a bookstagram theme to match, I can do that. It's fun for me to have the challenge of creating pics I wouldn't have set up for myself, and hopefully it takes some of the pressure off for authors who have a lot of other stuff on their plate.

All the packages come with a write-up that walks you step-by-step through a couple of my simple set-ups, similar to some of the tips I have in my story highlights, as an added little bit of support for anyone just starting out with taking bookstagram pics.

You can find Cherry Pie Author Services on Instagram at: @cherrypieauthorservices

Chapter 3: BOOKSTAGRAM vs AUTHOR ACCOUNTS

So, now you have an Instagram account, but what's your strategy going to be? How do you want to present yourself to the Instagram world?

I must emphasize that whichever account style you choose, it's not a personal Instagram account. This isn't where you post photos of your kids to make your parents happy, or selfies from your girls' night. If you already have an account like that (and I do), just start a new one for your author business. Instagram makes it really easy to switch between accounts, just keep 'em separated (shout-out to my fellow 90s teenagers).

Okay, so it's not a personal account. Then what do you post about? In my research, I've come across two main styles of accounts that work well. Bookstagram and what I call Author accounts. In my research, most successful authors on Instagram use one or a mix of these two styles. I really recommend that you check out the accounts in the interviews scattered throughout this book. I've labeled each of them as an author account or a bookstagram account. So what's the difference?

Author Accounts:

An author account is about you and your books. The goal is to create deeper relationships with your readers by giving them a greater connection to you and your life. You should have posts about your books, your upcoming books, and your writing process. Graphics with quotes and teasers are a great idea.

You can also share parts of your life that your readers would be interested in. What that includes is up to you, but I would aim for things that are part of your brand. If you write books with interesting settings, share travel photos that inspired your locations. If you write teashop cozies, share about your love of tea. Pets are always a great idea, but whenever possible, direct it back to your books. Things like your cat lying on your keyboard, or the walk with your dog that helped you work out an important plot point.

An author account isn't meant to represent your whole life. It's really about your books and the bits of your life that relate to your books. Also, we'll talk more about aesthetics later, but I would aim to only post photos that are cohesive and attractive. It might feel a bit staged but it's really about creating a mood that ties into your stories and overall brand. Think of it as visual storytelling.

Choose an author account if:

- You already have a dedicated fan base who want more ways to engage with you.

- You write in a genre that's not heavily followed by the bookstagram community.

- You want to get a bit more personal with your Instagram account.

- You're not afraid of self promotion.

Bookstagram:

Bookstagram is how I got my start, and I have a lot of affection for this little corner of the internet. Bookstagram is quite simply Books + Instagram. It's a community of readers sharing books they love or are excited about. The majority of the bookstagram community is made up of readers, but I met many of my author friends there, too.

I realize I'm talking about bookstagram like it's a place, or at the very least its own app, but it is, of course, still Instagram. You can find this corner of Instagram by searching hashtags (obviously, start with #bookstagram). Once you find some accounts that you like, see what hashtags they use and which accounts they interact with. My bookstagram account only follows other bookstagram accounts, author accounts, and some artists that I admire. When I log onto Instagram, I'm logging into that community.

The bookstagram community is mainly female, and mostly 20-40 year olds. I am one of the older ones at 38, and there are a handful of teenagers. So, the books that do well on bookstagram appeal to this demographic. There is a lot of YA, and the most popular books have a strong romantic subplot.

You might mainly sell ebooks, but print books are king on bookstagram, and a beautiful cover will create a lot of buzz. Remember, people are taking photos of books as a hobby, so they want photogenic books.

Fandom is a huge part of bookstagram. People love to talk about their favorite worlds, characters, and couples. There is a whole industry of candles, bookmarks, and even bath bombs that tie into the most loved books and series.

If you want to start a bookstagram account, you will be posting photos of books, and not just your books. Bookstagrammers are readers and community members first, authors second. I would recommend posting at least two photos of other books for every one of yours.

There are two advantages to this strategy. First of all, you will likely draw more attention with a post about a popular book. Choose books that you honestly enjoy, and that you think your ideal readers would enjoy. I write fairytale retellings with fae. So, I post a lot of fairytales and fae books. I also post a lot of general YA fantasy. All of those will hopefully attract readers who might also enjoy my books.

I mean, I also occasionally post about Red Rising and The Stormlight Archive, because I'm only human. But I get the most benefit from other books in my genre.

The second advantage to being a reader first is that it's easier to build relationships. Gushing about your favorite books—the part that made you cry, the romance that made you swoon—makes you relatable. It helps readers get to know you and see things they have in common with you. It builds relationships, and relationships sell books.

Choose a bookstagram account if:

- You are just starting out in your author career.

- You write in a genre that does well on bookstagram. These are Fantasy (especially YA), Scifi (again, especially YA), Romance (Romcoms do better than bodice rippers, but I'm seeing more and more romance in general), and to some extent, Thrillers.

- You'd rather soft sell (you still have to self promo though, or else this is just a hobby)

- You're less comfortable being the face of your brand, or you use a pen name.

Remember, you can always change later. My booksta-gram account gave my career a great start, but I am plan-ning to slowly shift it to being more about me and my own books as time goes on and I gain more readers. And, of course, some accounts are a blend of both styles.

Personal vs Private

Everyone has different comfort levels with how much of their lives they like to share online, as you'll see in the interviews. It's important to be genuine and authentic in your interactions, but that doesn't mean you need to share every bit of your life/struggles/feelings online. I like to share things that I would be happy to discuss with another parent on the playground, or someone on the bus. I'm not going to tell them where I live, but I'm very willing to discuss topics I think are important, like mental health or creative struggles.

Being real and connecting with your followers is important, but choosing what you share doesn't make you fake. It's just having boundaries. And where you set those boundaries is up to you.

INTERVIEW WITH: *Kim Chance*

Handle: @kimwritesbooks
Followers: 10.8k
Account style: Author
Genre: YA Contemporary Fantasy

How long have you been on Instagram, and where were you in your publishing journey when you started?
I started my author account back in July of 2015. At that point, I was still drafting what would eventually become my debut novel.

Do you feel that Instagram helps you sell books? How else is it helpful to you as an author?

I think Instagram is a great way to get your book out there, especially since it's a visual platform. I do think there is a good chance that readers who see the book will consider picking up a copy, especially if they really like the cover and see other people posting about it. However, I'm not sure Instagram really moves the needle in terms of sales from a broad standpoint. I'm traditionally published and while authors are often expected and asked to do their own marketing, I think the thing that really determines how well a book will do is how much marketing the publisher does on their end.

That being said, of all the social media platforms, I think Instagram is a great tool to showcase your work, and bookstagram is such a big deal now that it certainly can't hurt!

Instagram is also a really great place for authors to connect with fellow authors. Writing can be very solitary at times, so it's really nice to be involved with the writing community on Insta. In those moments when the writing gets really hard, it's nice to know we're not alone!

Which posts get the most engagement for you?

This might sound a little silly, but the posts that get the most engagement are selfies! I think it's because whenever I post a picture of myself, I'm usually opening up and being a bit more personal in the caption. My audience tends to really like that. I think they appreciate getting to know me on a more personal level, so those posts tend to get the most comments and likes.

What's your favorite thing about the community?
For the most part, I find Instagram to be a really positive, supportive place. There are exceptions of course, but overall, I have found it to be far more enjoyable and less stressful than other platforms. I also really love looking at all the pretty pictures. It amazes me some of the pictures bookstagrammers are putting out these days. There is so much talent out there, and I love scrolling through and getting to see it!

Do you have a strategy for balancing the sort of posts you make?
Not really. I do try to have a nice mix of reading, writing, and personal posts since my audience is a diverse group of folks, but overall, I just try to be super organic with my feed. Whatever I feel like posting is usually what

gets posted. That's probably not the best strategy, but I want my Instagram to be something that brings me joy—not something I'm super hyped up or stressed over.

What do you take your photos with? Do you use any editing software?

I just use my iPhone. I have a nice camera, but it's just so much easier to use my phone since my favorite editing software is actually an app. I'm a mom of three, so time is a pretty precious commodity for me. I'm always looking for ways to do things faster and more efficiently. Plus, I really like the portrait setting iPhone has for their cameras, and I use the VSCO editing app. I have a filter that I use and apply to all my photos.

Do you take your photos in batches, or do you take them and post them immediately?

I used to take them daily, but that eventually became too difficult to maintain. Now, I batch them! I try to take at least two weeks' worth of photos at a time. I pre-write most of my captions, and I use Planoly to schedule the posts. Planoly is really great because it allows you to see a preview of what your feed will look like with all the pictures added to it. It's super handy and makes the maintenance of my account so much easier!

How personal do you get on your account?

It depends on the topic! I'm a pretty open book when it comes to all things writing. I love meeting fellow writers, and I enjoy sharing my publishing journey with others. In terms of my personal life, I think it depends on the topic. For example, I'm an anxiety sufferer, and I'm really passionate about mental health awareness. It's something I talk about a lot on my feed.

But, in regards to my family and more specifics about my personal life, I keep all of that private. Privacy and safety, particularly where my children are concerned, is a huge priority so I keep everything family related off my account.

How much time do you devote to Instagram in a day or week?

I check it daily, but I really try to limit my time on Insta to a few hours a week. It's hard though—it's easy to get sucked in!

Do you have any advice for authors on using Instagram?

I think my best advice is to work on making your feed aesthetically cohesive. Since it's a visual platform, you want people to be able to tell it's your account just by looking at the photos you post. Having a theme just makes your account look more professional and pleasing to the eye. You don't have to get super elaborate with it, but something as simple as applying the same filter to each photo can make a big difference.

Also, engagement is huge. It's important to remember that there are thousands of accounts on Instagram, and if someone takes the time to comment on yours, then do your best to comment back. Plus, this is really good for the algorithm. If you're looking to grow your account, engagement is key.

And have fun! Life's too short to stress over social media!

Chapter 4: CREATING A COHESIVE FEED

A great post will get you likes and comments, but it's a great feed that will get you new followers. When someone checks out your profile after discovering a post of yours that they like, or following a link from elsewhere on the internet, it's usually the style of your feed that draws them in. Your feed should match the feel of your overall brand, and of your books.

In bookstagram, we call the look of our feeds our "theme." This can feel a bit inauthentic if you're used to posting unplanned images, but remember, the goal is visual storytelling. We want to draw people into the world of our books. Here are some ways to think about the look of your feed:

Colors:

A quick way to create a cohesive theme is to have a color scheme. Pick a few colors that you like—and go well with your book covers—and search for props and settings that have those colors.

My feed currently has a lot of pale backgrounds and rainbow books. I'm heavy on pink, yellow, and turquoise. It's unapologetically girly. I add pops of color with ribbons that I use as bookmarks, a couple of bright dresses that I wear in photos, and flowers in pinks and yellows. Nothing fancy or expensive.

Mood:

Your feed should have a mood that suits your brand. My feed is light and airy. Lots of twinkle lights and fresh flowers. But maybe your brand is more earthy, dark and moody, modern and shiny, cozy, or whimsical.

If you're not sure what your look should be, think hard about the tone of your books, and the things you naturally gravitate toward. Then spend some time looking through other Instagram feeds that you think are attractive. Screenshot the feeds you like best and see what similarities there are between them. Are they mostly outside? Very dark? Are the photos cluttered and full of interesting things to look at, or minimalist and simple? All these things tie into the overall mood of your feed.

Editing and Filters:

It's up to you how far you want to fall into the photo-editing rabbit hole, but stick to a similar way of editing all your photos. Filters are effects you can apply either in Instagram or often in photo editing apps. If you use the same filter for all your photos, it will add a lot of cohesiveness to your feed. If you pull a lot of very different photos into your feed, running them through a more dramatic filter can make them look like they belong together.

I'm a photographer so I edit my photos on my computer in Lightroom or Photoshop, instead of using filters. This is more work but gives me more control over the look of my photos. I edit my bookstagram photos more heavily than my personal photography, as I've found that browsers like a more "filtered" look. But some accounts do better with more natural, unedited photos, so it's good to experiment. In the end, you need to pick a look that you can stick to and enjoy!

Photos vs graphics:

Okay, so what about using non-photo images? Graphics with quotes or book sales? I see these used more effectively on author accounts than bookstagram, and they need to match your feed as well. They should tie into the colors and mood of your photos. I will caution you that graphics typically get less engagement than photos, but I know they can be useful.

Arranging your posts:

If you are posting more than one type of image, or using photos and graphics, it can help to plan out the order of your posts ahead of time. This is a great reason to use a planning app (I have a couple listed in the Resources section at the back of the book). Take some photos in advance and play with their arrangement to see what you like.

If you alternate two types of images, they will show up as a checkerboard, which can be fun. You can also alternate between three types of images, which will organize your grid into vertical stripes.

I currently only use photos, but I have four styles and alternate them to create a grid that is balanced but less obviously planned looking.

Collages and Theme Dividers:

Sometimes you'll see someone on Instagram post a larger graphic split into separate images, so that if you look at their feed, the photos combine to make a large image. This can be really dramatic, but I don't recommend it if you're planning to post regularly (which I hope you will!) because it's hard to keep all those posts lined up. You'd have to always post three times in a row to keep the grid from shifting and the image looking messy.

Not only that, but the individual posts are just parts of an image and will be confusing for anyone who happens to come across them. You could maybe do this effectively for a cover reveal, but know that it will not help your overall feed.

Some people like to post a three image "theme divider" when they change up their theme, but I wouldn't recommend that either for the same reasons. You don't need to make a big fuss about changing your feed. Just change it.

How long should you keep a theme?

This is completely up to you. Some people change every month, and I've seen successful bookstagrammers with the exact same theme (in fact, nearly the exact same flat lay setup) for three years. Do what's easy for you and makes you a happy creative. If you change regularly, keep an eye on which of your themes seem to do best.

I change mine with the seasons, based on subtle shifts in things like natural light and availability of flowers. Come spring, I always switch to outdoor photos as I find it more inspiring, and in the fall, I take my feed back inside for cozy tea-and-candles shots.

If you admire a feed, go even deeper and scroll back to see how they've changed over the months and seasons, or if they've stayed pretty consistent over time.

INTERVIEW WITH: *Caroline George*

Handle: @authorcarolinegeorge
Followers: 15.9k
Account type: Author
Genre: YA

How long have you been on Instagram, and where were you in your publishing journey when you started?

I joined Instagram when I was in high school, but I started using the account for business purposes four to five years ago. At the time, I was still a new author with very little social media and branding knowhow. I learned over time, failed a lot, and slowly grew my audience into a book-centric following.

Dearest Josephine is coming out next year with Harper Collins. Do you think your social media platform was helpful in being picked up?

Yes! Platform is a huge part of landing book deals. Nowadays, publishers want to know authors can sell their own projects and engage with their targeted readership. Platform can include a bunch of things like mailing lists, organizational memberships, etc. However, in the YA space, social media plays the largest role in platform development.

I believe social media helped my books get through the metaphorical publishing door.

Can you tell us a bit about your cover reveal tour for Dearest Josephine? Is there anything you'd do differently next time?

I'll be honest – I didn't expect the tour to "blow up" as much as it did. I initiated the event by posting a general invitation on my Instagram story, asking if anyone wanted to participate in the reveal. I was overwhelmed by responses. The cover ended up reaching hundreds of thousands of people. Crazy!

For the tour, I offered participants a first-look at the cover, exclusive character wallpaper, and entry into a gift card giveaway.

Next time, I'll spend more time planning an actual tour!

How personal do you get on your account?

This is a great question! I think honesty and vulnerability are needed to build connections with followers. I try to be open about my publishing experiences and normal life. In contrast to that, I do set boundaries for my account. I don't post "personal" photos, i.e. ones with family and friends. I also don't share the intimate details of my day-to-day. Over the years, I've learned effective branding requires a healthy balance of transparency/personality and professionalism.

What sort of posts get the most engagement for you?

My followers tend to engage most with photos of me that have blog-style captions. Book layouts and pictures of inanimate objects receive very little engagement in my experience.

Overall, I believe the key to platform is community, and community requires some face-to-face interaction even if that interaction is via photos. My advice: Show your face. Share your voice. Be honest. And speak to the people you're trying to reach.

How much time do you devote to Instagram in a day or week?

Due to writing deadlines, I haven't been able to dedicate as much time to Instagram. I spend at least an hour on Instagram each day. Post creation requires several hours (to take the photo, edit it, and write the caption). After posting, I spend another hour engaging with people on the app to boost my appearance in the algorithm.

What do you take your photos with? Do you use any editing software?

I take most of my photos on my iPhone 8. I edit using Lightroom, sometimes PicArt and Visco. I plan my layouts via Planoly.

What are a couple of caption types or questions that you like best?

Easy-to-answer questions tend to get the most responses. For example, I asked if a photo looked more like Nancy Drew or Lorelai, and I received a ton of comments, more than usual.

People don't want to spend a lot of time commenting, but they do want to engage. So, asking whether your followers like coffee or tea would be better for engagement than asking them to share their favorite beach memory. Regarding caption types, I see the best results when I write captions like mini blogs.

What's your favorite thing about the author/bookstagram community?

People are so supportive! I've made amazing friends on the app, and I love how bookstagram helps connect readers to new books.

Do you have any advice for authors on using Instagram?

Social media is all about the followers! Some advice . . . Know your author brand. Who are you? What's your message, voice, color scheme? Why should people follow your account?

Be consistent! Quality over quantity. Make sure all your posts connect to your author brand and offer some sort of takeaway/call-to-action.

Community sells books! Anything you can do to welcome people into your journey will help foster platform growth and generate sales.

Launch or join an Instagram pod.* Do giveaways. Team up with other accounts.
Pinpoint where your target audience (possible readers) hang out and work to reach them.

Set aside time each week to write your captions and curate photo content. I can't easily switch from "social media brain" to "writer brain," so I give myself one or two mornings each week to prepare my social media content.

*for more on pods, check out the Engagement section!

Chapter 5: PHOTOGRAPHY

Photography is the heart of Instagram, but it's also one of the hardest things to tackle in a non-visual guide like this. To really get a feel for photography, you'll need to experiment and learn. I came into Instagram already a photographer, but it's a skill that can be learned and you don't need a lot of expensive gear to do it. You can certainly use the camera on your phone, and the filters Instagram provides, and come up with some great photos. It's all about knowing the limitations of your gear, and having good light.

Equipment

You need a camera that takes good, clear photos. A lot of phones will do the trick. I have a cheap phone and I only use it for Stories, not feed photos because it doesn't take nice photos. Start with what you have, but know that nice quality photos always do better on Instagram. You'll see in the interviews that a lot of the accounts I feature take photos with their phones.

You might assume that you *need* to use your phone for the photos, but Instagram allows you to upload images saved onto your phone (you can email them to yourself), through a planning app, or using Facebook Creator Studio, so I recommend using the best camera you have at your disposal. Whatever you shoot with, you need to know what sort of photos your camera can handle best.

The camera on a phone requires good lighting to not be blurry or grainy. Most also won't have the same options for depth of field that a DSLR (a digital camera with swappable lenses) has. So, you may not be able to get that nice blurry background that isolates your subject.

However, phone cameras are great for scenic photos, and shots where you want the background to be in focus. Any camera can pull off a good flat lay (a photo taken from directly above objects on a flat surface), which is part of the reason that style of photo is so popular.

If you are wanting an upgrade from your phone camera, the Canon Rebels are a great choice, and the 50 1.8 prime lens is inexpensive but has great glass.

Light

There's a saying that goes like this: Amateur photographers look at the subject, intermediate photographers look at the background, but professional photographers look at the light.

Light is what makes or breaks your photos, whether you want an artistic glowy shot or just a crisp, clear photo. You'll want to pay attention to the light in your house, yard, and anywhere else you think would be fun to take photos. Watch how it changes throughout the day and the year. Experiment with different locations and times of day and see what gives you a result you like.

If your house is bright, don't shoot in direct sunlight. You want filtered light. That could mean taking a flat lay photo just beside that bright patch of sunlight on your floor, not in it. Or it might mean hanging sheer curtains or a white sheet over your giant living room window to diffuse the harsh shadows and reflections. You also might want to pick a time of day when the room is bright, but doesn't have sun shining directly in.

If your house is darker, think about windowsills, or your entryway with the door wide open. You can also use twinkle lights and candles to add light if you want a cozy, moody look. I shift around to different areas in my house as the light changes throughout the year

I also use a reflector more often in lower light. This can be an actual photographer's reflector, a piece of white foam core from the dollar store, or even those foil reflectors you put in your car window in the summer. The idea is to place the reflector on the darker side of your set-up. The light will bounce off the reflector and brighten the shadows on that side, creating a more even look. This is especially helpful for flat lays.

If you want to shoot outdoors, it's all about being not too bright and not too dark. Look for bright overcast days, or light filtered through trees and shrubs. If you want that beautiful golden glow, aim to shoot photos just after the sun rises, or just before it sets. I must confess that I never take sunrise photos. I'm not an early bird!

Backgrounds

If possible, avoid pure white backdrops. They might seem like a good idea, but they are difficult to photograph well. Aim for light gray or cream if you want a light neutral backdrop. Pure black is also tricky. As a general rule (in all photography), it's easier to get a good photo if you avoid black, white, bright orange, bright red, and fluorescent pink. All of those will confuse your poor camera and you'll end up with a photo that has a funky color balance. What you want are midtones.

Some bookstagrammers use purchased backdrops—vinyl sheets with wood planks, marble, or other patterns printed on them. They look very realistic in photos.

I prefer to use blankets for my flat lays, and my house and yard for other photos. It's all about the style you like best. You can use walls (I take photos with my gallery wall in the background), bookcases, beds, tables, a wooden floor, or go on location to a cafe, bookstore, or take a hike in the woods.

Props

Anything can be a prop!

Choose props that work with your branding and genre. You don't have to spend a lot of money, and you might have everything you need at home. I use a lot of teacups and fresh flowers along with a variety of ribbons in colors that match my brand. I have neutral blankets and baskets for texture. My house plants sometimes sneak into photos, as does my cat (I bribe him into shots with chamomile tea. People love seeing your pets). I did buy a couple crowns off Amazon to go with my fairytale theme. Here are some prop ideas. Maybe some of them are lurking around your house right now!

- Beverages: tea/coffee, cups, pots, kettles, iced drinks, alcohol
- Snacks: colorful treats, pastries, cupcakes, fruit, candy, waffles
- Kitchen items: baskets, cutting boards, china, cake stands, wooden spoons
- Nature: flowers, leaves, ferns, moss, faux butterflies, feathers, sticks, houseplants, silk or dried flowers, pinecones, gems, rocks
- Textiles: blankets, quilts, rugs
- Clothing: socks, sweaters, cute shoes, slippers, scarves, glasses
- Lights: candles, twinkle lights, little fairy lights.
- Hobbies: notepads, journals, pens, paintbrushes, balls of yarn, typewriters and cameras

- Fun: crowns, toys (Funko Pops are popular), old keys, swords/daggers/letter openers

- Words: Scrabble tiles, letter boards, calligraphy, printed paper

- Pops of color: ribbons, scrapbook paper, fabric

- Bookish merchandise: bookmarks, pins, stickers, character art, book sleeves

- More books: stacks, rainbows, open books, shelves

I'm always on the lookout for new ideas to keep things fresh. I love being inspired by other people's photos and I keep a saved folder on Instagram for shots that I might want to try to replicate in my own way.

INTERVIEW WITH: *Sarah Moore*

Handle: @newleafwriter

Followers: 46.6k

Account style: Bookstagram (influencer & Etsy shop owner)

When did you start your account?

I started way back in 2015.

Which posts get the most engagement for you?

Shelfies (photos of bookshelves) and photos of my craft space.

What's your favorite thing about the community?
Definitely making friends with whom I chat in DMs, although I also really like the aesthetic aspect. I enjoy scrolling through my feed and liking what I see. My account also helps funnel people toward my Etsy shop.

What do you take your photos with? Do you use any editing software?
I take all my photos with my phone and edit them in the Lightroom app.

Do you take your photos in batches, or do you take them and post them immediately?
Always in batches.

What are a couple of caption types or questions that you like best?
I like to ask people about the small stuff and the big stuff, if you will. The small stuff includes what they had for breakfast, when they got up that morning, what their favorite color is. The big stuff includes questions like the role of science or literature in human advancement, our duties toward changing racism (especially a problem

here in America, but more generally everywhere), and considerations about the environment. While the latter question types typically generate far fewer responses, I still think they are important as someone with a platform to ask.

How do you choose if you're going to promote a book?
Typically, I promote a book if I'm really interested in it and if the author is willing to send me a physical copy as I'm not an ebook reader.

Do you have any tips for authors in creating a cohesive theme?
Choose only a few colors and stick to them, choose a few basic setups and stick to those as well, and confine your interests as much as possible. That way, the people who follow you will be superfans. Superfans are worth much more than a larger following. For instance, I have more than 45k followers, but only about 200 of them shop my Etsy site or comment regularly.

Some have even become my pen pals. That's who you want to reel in, and you can do so by giving them regular content that meets a pretty narrow aesthetic and content standard.

To learn in more detail about how Sarah succeeds at Instagram, check out her course at: https://newleaf-writing.teachable.com/p/Instagram-and-bookstagram

Chapter 6: SELFIES

It can be hard to decide how personal to be on social media. Some people choose to only post photos of books, but it can be hard to build relationships if people don't have a face to connect with your account. I'm a big fan of authors posting selfies.

If you have a super-secret pen name, maybe this doesn't apply to you, but for everyone else, I would suggest you post an occasional photo of yourself on your feed. One where people can see your face. Because people are more likely to buy things from people they know and like, and it's much harder to know and like someone whose face you've never seen.

I know a lot of people are camera shy, and I totally understand. If you don't generally like photos of yourself, here are some tips.

1) Take a lot of photos, and pick the best one. This is one of the reasons I use a timer instead of having someone else take my pictures. It's easier to take twenty photos if I'm not harassing someone else to do it.

2) Take photos from a level or high angle. If the camera is lower than your face, it'll make you look larger. If it's at eye level, you'll look the way you look, and if it's looking down, you'll look smaller. Now, I'm not advocating you hold your camera straight above you just to look slimmer, but if you let your five-year-old take your photo, you may not be happy with the results. And if you have your ten-year-old take your photo, maybe get them to stand on a box.

3) Smiling at the camera is nice, and it makes you look friendly. But if you feel silly doing it, or just aren't in the mood, then take a more lifestyle approach and take a photo casually reading a book or writing in a journal.

4) If you're trying to keep a consistent color scheme, try wearing something that matches your feed, or take a photo against a similar background. You could also be

holding or hanging out with a prop that you often use (teacups, skulls, your dog, whatever).

You don't need to look like a supermodel for your photo to be a good marketing tool. Just show your followers that you're a real human every now and then, and they will love you for it. And the more you see yourself in photos, the more natural it will feel.

INTERVIEW WITH: *Kealan Patrick Burke*

Handle: @kealanpatrick
Followers: 4.9k
Account style: Author
Genre: Horror

How long have you been on Instagram, and where were you in your publishing journey when you started?
I joined Instagram in the summer of 2017. By then, I'd published over two dozen books and roughly two hundred short stories. So I was well along the path.

Do you feel that Instagram helps you sell books? How else is it helpful to you as an author?

It very much does help sell books, particularly via the #Bookstagram community, whose love and enthusiasm for books is, to my mind, unrivalled on any other social platform. Because Instagram is primarily visual, every review or mention comes with a picture of your book, the equivalent of having it facing out on shelves in bookstores.

Write a good enough book that strikes a chord within the community, and everyone will want to buy it, read it, and photograph it for themselves, especially (and often only) if the cover art is good. As an author, I love seeing how creative readers get with their photographs. It's very rarely just a flat picture of the book. Bookstagrammers create their own art, and it's wonderful to behold. That level of enthusiasm and love is also incredibly encouraging for a writer who may be in the doldrums with a project.

Do you do anything special for a book launch on Instagram?

Other than giveaways and incentives, I usually just write up a post about the book and take a good picture of it, something that gives you the best idea of what it's about. Bookstagrammers often take that ball and run with it, which is why it's an invaluable asset for me. Outside of that, I ensure the book has gone to reviewers, and has enough buzz prior to release day. Instagram alone is not enough for a successful launch, at least not for me, but it's terrific for getting people talking, and the cumulative effect over time is worth gold.

Which posts get the most engagement for you?
Selfies of me with my books, pictures of my dog, and pictures of dishes I've cooked, in that order. :)

What's your favorite thing about the Instagram community?
Their creativity. Also, as mentioned above, the enthusiasm the #Bookstagram community has for books and reading has often reignited my own passion for writing on days when the words were slow to come. They're inspiring and endlessly supportive, and I don't think they get nearly enough credit for that. They're also a hell of a lot of fun :)

Do you have a strategy for balancing the sort of posts you make?

I try to have a good balance of things: my books, my dog, cooking, my travels and misadventures, and other random things to make it interesting. Nobody wants seven selfies of me in a row. It looks narcissistic. And endlessly posting about my books gets old, too. It's important to have a personality on there and any other social media platform. If it's just a billboard for the things you're selling, you can expect people to keep driving right on by. Variety is fun, monotony isn't.

How personal do you get on your account?

If I get personal, it's usually via humor. I like to share when funny things happen to me. Otherwise, I keep a distinct boundary between my writing persona and the "real" me. I think that's important. You can't share everything or the relationship between writer and reader gets complicated and sometimes a little weird.

How much time do you devote to Instagram in a day or week?

Only as much as necessary. I'm pretty good at responding to people's comments and messages, but I try to limit my social media to an hour or two a day. Any more than that and I'm just blatantly trying to avoid doing any work. Other days, I don't post at all. I know all advice says you should post something every day, but I'm not that disciplined and often don't feel like posting just for the sake of it.

Do you have any advice for authors on using Instagram?
Don't treat it like it exists to sell your book for you or make you famous. Bring some personality to it. Nobody wants to see an Instagram that's just a wall of your book covers. Don't message people with a link to your book when they follow you back. It's amateurish and annoying and will get you blocked. Nobody likes being spammed.

Engage with your readers and don't treat them like they're there to do you a service. You're the author. You're there to entertain them. And above all else, have fun. If you have to be on social media at all, make sure it's not just all work, all the time. Let go and enjoy yourself. Enjoy the connection with people who love what you do. Otherwise, what's the point?

Chapter 7: PLANNING YOUR POSTS

I post photos every day, but I do not—I repeat—do not take photos every day! Some people like to be spontaneous, but I'm a planner. Also, I make a mess taking photos and if I did it daily, the stacks of books around my house would never get tidied up. Unlike now, when they totally do...

I take five or so photos at a time. So, once a week I'll put aside an hour or two and take a bunch of photos. I usually set up a nice little spot and take multiple photos, just switching the books and rearranging my props slightly. It's not a bad thing to have photos that look really similar. It helps keep a cohesive look to your feed.

Then I edit the photos using Adobe Lightroom on my computer and organize them in my Instagram folder for the month. I like to have photos done in advance so that I can balance my feed aesthetically, and taking photos at the same time gives a nice consistency to my feed. It also helps me take advantage of days with good light, which can be a struggle when British Columbia gets rainy.

Currently, I just save all my edited photos into the folder and arrange them by numbering the photos. In the past, I've used planning apps that let you see your grid in advance. I love that, but it's more convenient for me to skip that step, and I have a good idea by now how to keep things balanced.

People have different ways to create a cohesive theme. Some people take all their photos the exact same way, like all flat lays with the same props, or all outdoors under the same mossy tree. That way they all match. Some people take all sorts of photos but use the same filters so that the colors all sort of go together. Some people choose to alternate photos with graphics.

You might also want to come up with your captions ahead of time. If you use Facebook's Creator Studio or a grid planning app, you can save your posts as drafts and have them ready to go. If you're more comfortable working on your computer than your phone, I really recommend trying out Creator Studio, so that you can do everything on your computer. Even if you come up with your captions as you post, be sure to save them somewhere first in case the post fails to go through. It can be very frustrating to retype everything!

In addition to keeping my feed pretty, I also think about these things when planning my feed:

- How often am I posting my own books? (about 25% of the time in my case, as I'm a bookstagrammer, not an author account)

- Have I shown my face lately?

- Am I regularly posting about popular books that relate to my book?

- Are there any cover reveals or book releases that I offered to help my fellow authors with?

I also balance rep posts and participate in monthly challenges, which I'll explain in more detail in parts four and five!

All this depends on your personality and how you want to use Instagram, but I like having things planned out. It's less to think about day to day, which frees up my brain to do other creative work.

Post Ideas

But still, what to post about? I've scoured Instagram for as many post ideas as I could find. Don't say I never gave you anything.

Daily Themed Posts:

These are some hashtags that you can build a post around.

#mugmonday

#moodboardmonday

#mapmonday (as a map maker, I post this one a lot!)

#mermaidmonday (often used by artists, but I say, post all the mermaid books)

#teatuesday

#tolkientuesday

#wickwednesday (wick as in candles)

#waitingonwednesday (an upcoming release you're excited for)

#throwbackthursday (#tbt for the lazy. Just kidding. Use both)

#followfriday (tag people you want others to follow)

#fantasyonfriday

#stacksaturday (also #bookstacksaturday)

#caturday (cat+Saturday)

#socksunday

#shelfiesunday (a shelfie is a photo of your book-shelf)

And yes, you must use those hashtags. Hashtags are important. See Chapter 8.

Other ideas:

- TBR stack. The books you plan to read that week, month…or year? I don't know how fast you read

- meet the author/Instagrammer post (even though this is about you, still ask your followers a question)

- book you're currently reading

- book you enjoyed (or a negative review, but try to be a positive human)

- bookish fanart

- you reading a book

- your kid reading a book

- your cat/dog/hamster reading a book (or sleeping on it, whatever they like to do)

- cool vacation spots. With a book (are you sensing a theme? Always with a book)
- upcoming books you're super excited for
- your writing workspace
- journals or post-its, or however you plan your books
- your bookshelves (bonus points for rainbow bookshelves. I know some people don't like them, but they get more engagement for me!)
- books with tea/coffee/snacks
- your rough maps/character art/cover ideas
- bookmarks and bookswag
- dress up like a book character

These are just to help you get your creative juices flowing. As always, follow other authors and bookstagrammers and get inspiration from their ideas!

INTERVIEW WITH: *C.E. Clayton*

Handle: @chelscey
Followers: 1.8k
Account style: Author/Bookstagram
Genre: Fantasy/Cyberpunk

How long have you been on Instagram, and where were you in your publishing journey when you started?

I technically started my Instagram account as a personal account (reluctantly, I might add) in 2013 or so I believe? I didn't convert my personal account to an author platform until about 2017, and that's when I started to more actively use my account for my books and my primary author platform. That was also the time my first book in my Monster of Selkirk series came out, which is late for when you're "supposed" to start building your platforms.

My Instagram handle has never changed though since I first started—sometimes it helps to have a unique spelling of your name. I'm really easy to find now! I also still have the ability to branch out and show off my other interests beyond writing and books, as my handle isn't hyper specific, but is still very representative of who I am now as an author.

Do you feel that Instagram helps you sell books? How else is it helpful to you as an author?

It does! There is a very vibrant community on Instagram for book lovers: bookstagram. Finding that community and being a part of it allowed me to get my work in front of the very audience that not only loves to read, but loves to gush and show off these gorgeous photos of books and share their reviews in such a positive way. This was especially true with my latest book launch where working with other bookstagrammers got my book into the hands of some really talented influencers, who then introduced my book to their thousands of followers who love to find out about new books.

One of the other ways it's helped me is through the author community. Through Instagram I was able to meet other authors and writers and join writing groups, find beta readers, and overall just talk to people who have similar struggles as I do. Finding that solidarity was very important because, while I love my family dearly, they don't often get what it's like to be a writer or how to publish a book. The community that I found through Instagram got me in touch with people I could ask questions to, get support from, and it's turned even the most frustrating or lonely aspects of writing into something more enjoyable.

Do you do anything special for a book launch on Instagram?

I've done everything from bookstagram tours for book launches, to my own personal giveaways where I'll give away art or a signed book if people like and share and comment on my launch day post. I really like doing the Instagram Live recording for launches. Not only is it a special treat for those who can join you, but you're able to save the video afterward as well so those who couldn't attend can still watch and engage. It's a special event that keeps on giving even after launch day is done! I vary what I do so, hopefully, no two book launches feel identical, which gives my followers something new to look forward to with each new book.

Do you have any advice for authors on using Instagram?
Be consistent. Whether that's in posting every day at a certain time, or keeping to a set theme for every photo, just showing up and providing the content is the hardest thing. If you only post once a month or when you have a new book coming out, you won't grow your platform, you won't gain a following, which means you won't have anyone to share your work with. Instagram is work, and sometimes that work is draining and it won't be fun, but consistency is what helped me build an audience even with the constant changes that roll out on the platform.

What's helped me most is to not take pictures the same day I post them. So I'll take a months' worth of photos and videos in one day. I will set aside the whole day to do that, so that on days when I am busy with actually writing my books, I still have something I can share and I don't have to spend hours staging or editing a photo, because I already did it.

I also have a scheduling app which lets me schedule my posts. It's been a life saver in saving me time and avoiding social media burnout, so I definitely recommend something like that if you're worried about the time commitment social media can take.

Engage with the community. Comment on other's posts that you admire, be genuine in your comments, and you'll be surprised by how many people will engage with you in return. The rest can get really technical of what kind of hashtags to use, whether you should join an engagement group, what times of the day to post, who to follow and what not, but that can be really overwhelming, and what works for me and the kind of books I write may not be the same for another author.

Which posts get the most engagement for you?

The kinds of posts that get the most likes and comments are generally the ones where I show my face in some capacity. People seem to like my candor when I tend to show my face, and not because I do anything crazy with make-up or cosplaying either, but I think people, and readers in general, like seeing the face behind the bookstagrammer. They like feeling like they are getting to know the author by seeing them more regularly than just promotional photos or headshots. At least that has been my experience, but anytime I show my face and my crazy hair, or me and my dog, the engagement tends to be best all around for both likes and comments.

What's your favorite thing about the community?

The bookstagram community and the reading community in general on Instagram has been some of the nicest people and most supportive I've met on any other platform. Sure, there are its toxic moments and people, but generally speaking, it's been so refreshing to be on a section of the internet and social media that loves to celebrate stories and the people who write them. I have met a fantastic group of writers that I now am in a writer's group with, which has in turn helped me tremendously with writing my books.

I would never have met them without the book community on Instagram. And through them and my other author friends, I have found so many new books to fall in love with too! It's been amazing and really encouraging for an indie author to be a part of this community that it has become my preferred way of engaging with people.

Do you have a strategy for balancing the sort of posts you make?

By taking my photos and videos for the month all at once, it helps me maintain a kind of theme and vibe, because I have everything set up and I don't accidentally forget to use a certain prop like I do when I spread out taking my Instagram photos. But this strategy also means that every month I change up what I do a bit, so I don't get bored with taking photos!

So they go back and forth between purely book related posts such as: book reviews and asking questions on what people think of this book or that trope, etc. to more writing related content and offering strategies and advice on how to craft stories or seeking it in return. It helps me balance the two sides of my account as well, who I am as a reader and book reviewer, and who I am as a writer and storyteller.

How do you like to use Stories?

The way I most like using Stories is to showcase the things I do in my personal life that aren't maybe book or writing related at all. I use Stories to show the places I visit, or some of the cool things I'm doing, or the concerts I'm attending. I also use them to rant sometimes! But the Stories functionality, when I do use it, tends to be the most personal content I show. It's the realest version of myself and my hobbies and the things that bring me joy.

How personal do you get on your account?

As my following has grown, I don't post as much about my family or husband just because I want to respect their privacy as well. But, as I mentioned before with my Stories, I feel safer to be candid about the things I struggle with, the things I like doing, and the places I go to. I think it can be a disservice to my followers to only show perfectly crafted moments, so I like to get personal occasionally and I am always, ALWAYS blown away by how many messages I get after of people saying how much they agree with what I've shared, or appreciate that I feel the same as they do, or just enjoy the weird things I come across.

All this to say: don't be afraid to get deep and personal on your account sometimes! Your readers and followers do appreciate it, and your words may really help someone get through a tough time.

How much time do you devote to Instagram in a day or week?

I usually devote a good hour (on and off, of course) to Instagram every day. Maybe a bit less on weekends, but as I do try to post every day, I want to make sure I am engaging with others and responding to comments throughout the day. Usually at the end of the month, I spend more time with Instagram just because those are also the days I take a bunch of new photos and get those edited and scheduled for the following month.

Chapter 8: HASHTAGS

Hashtags can get a bad rap on other platforms, and for good reason. They're often used just to emphasis a point (#blessed) or to be funny (#TimeToBuyMoreCookies), which is not amusing to everyone. But don't ignore hashtags on Instagram. They're what the system runs on. Hashtags are Instagram's keywords. Every hashtag creates its own feed on Instagram which you can view by clicking it. If you're using hashtags well, you'll get people viewing your posts through those hashtag feeds.

If it's a hashtag no one uses, then no one else will click on it and see your posts. If it's a hashtag that thousands of people use every day, then it's unlikely that anyone will see your posts, because it will immediately get buried under the sheer onslaught of #books. It's best to pick something in the middle, that's specific to what you're posting about, and is used by the community you want to reach. Generally, about a third of my views are from hashtags, and for a post that does really well, it will be about half the views. That's not a small thing. You need to use hashtags.

How many should I use?

You're allowed to use thirty. So, you should use thirty. Every hashtag is another path to your feed. The more paths, the better. Instagram does not punish you for using more or less hashtags, so just use the full amount.

Okay, then what hashtags should I use?

I'm so glad you asked! Here's some ideas:

- the author, book title, and series title. This also counts if it's your own book. Even if no one else is posting yet, they will be! So, I use: #hannasandvig #therosegate #faerietaleromances.

- the genre of the book: #scifi #fantasy #yafantasy #contemporaryromance #scarybooks #christianfiction #ireadya

- hashtags that describe your photo: #rainbowbookstack #bookishselfie #booksandswords #fantasymaps #shelfie

- hashtags used by communities outside of the book community that intersect with your photo: #plantmom #gingercatsofInstagram #teasnobsunite #aquietmoment

- author hashtags: #amwriting #indieauthorsofInstagram #authorslife #authorsupportingauthors

- bookstagram hashtags: #booksbooksbooks #booknerdigans #bookdragon #bookaesthetic #bibliophile #readersofig #idratherbereading

To find more hashtags, follow people who do well on Instagram and check out what hashtags they use. They will either be at the bottom of the caption—often under a stack of dots—or in their first comment. Both places work for you as well, by the way.

It can be handy to keep a list. Some Instagram layout apps let you save them, or you can start a document. I have a document that I copy/paste from and I'll also check previous posts I've made with similar content. This is easy to do if you use Facebook Creator to post, because you can do it on your computer.

Keep it fresh, don't just reuse the same hashtags for three years. Each hashtag is a new potential audience, so rotate through them. If a hashtag has become really popular, it might be less effective for you, and there are always new ones popping up. It's a good idea to do a little sleuthing through other people's hashtags every month or two, to see what's being used in the community.

There are also a few services you can use to find hashtags. You have to take them with a grain of salt—an AI can't tell the difference between fiction books and bookkeeping—but you can get some fresh hashtags that way. Three free websites I found for hashtags are: https://www.all-hashtag.com, https://displaypurposes.com, and https://ingramer.com. I especially liked how Ingramer rates hashtags from most to least popular, as it's a good strategy to have a mix of popular and less used hashtags.

Banned hashtags

You also need to watch for banned hashtags. Occasionally, a seemingly benign hashtag will be banned due to too many posts using that hashtag that go against Instagram's Terms of Service. If you use a banned hashtag, that post won't show up on hashtag feeds, Explore, or search pages. Sometimes if you use a banned hashtag, you can get "shadow banned" which means that none of your posts show up anywhere, even the ones without the hashtag. I found this out when I used the hashtag #romance when posting about a romance novel. Don't use #romance! If you end up with a banned hashtag, you'll need to figure out which one it is and delete it from all your posts.

You can check to see if a hashtag is banned using a website like https://iqhashtags.com/banned-hashtags.

INTERVIEW WITH: *Harriet Young*

Handle: @thesenovelthoughts

Followers: 35.5k

Account style: Bookstagram

Genre: Historical Thriller

(crowdsourced through Unbound)

How long have you been on Instagram, and where were you in your publishing journey when you started?

I've been on Instagram for 3.5 years. I started it as a "writer" Instagram rather than a "reader" Instagram, but over a very short period it switched to the latter. At the time, I was training to become a teacher, and my novel was in its infancy. The course was challenging, and my account and writing were an outlet. The focus switched to reading, and that was how it stayed until early 2019, when my novel was finally finished.

Your upcoming book, The Hellion, was successfully funded through Unbound, which uses a crowdsourcing model to publish books. What was that process like?
The process was difficult, heart-breaking, heart-warming, crushing and joyful all at once - often all of these things in the same day! I learned very quickly that if you don't ask, you don't get—but if you do ask, you can very easily be in the firing line of quite a lot of vitriol.

"Putting yourself out there" is, I think, difficult for most of us. It is particularly challenging for those of us with an innate response of self-deprecation. But the overwhelming outpouring of love and support was more than enough to (partially) bury that feeling. There were days when it went really well and days when it didn't quite go so well, but overall it was an experience that I will be forever grateful for.

Do you think your Instagram account helped you reach the pledge amount you needed to have your book published?

Absolutely. Without my wonderful followers pledging, I could never have reached the pledge amount. Their pledges amounted to over 75% of the total.

How did you leverage your Instagram to make people aware of your Unbound project?

I used a variety of methods. Of course, I shared my progress on my Stories and feed, but it is very easy to get audience fatigue by sharing too often. The best methods I found of driving awareness were giveaways, regular updates when the percentage increased, and direct messaging.

Do you have any tips for authors on Instagram who might be thinking of running a campaign on a crowdsourcing platform?

Don't worry about negativity. It happens. Shrug it off. Remember your end goal, and push. Find out what your followers respond well to, and just go for it! The vast majority of people are kind and will support your endeavours. Whatever way you choose to do it, though, keep it consistent. During my campaign, I was messaging people for around two hours a day. However much it might look easy, it usually isn't!

Which posts get the most engagement for you?

Giveaways always do well (of course) but also any photos featuring my cats!

What's your favorite thing about the community?

The absolute love of books and reading. People are fiercely passionate in the bookstagram community, and that is just a wonderful thing.

What do you take your photos with? Do you use any editing software?

I use a Canon camera and edit my photos with a Photoshop Express app. It's usually just cropping, increasing exposure (the brighter the photo, the better it does in my experience) and fiddling with colors.

Do you take your photos in batches, or do you take them and post them immediately?

At the moment, I take them and post immediately. In the depths of winter, I might utilize the light a little more and take a few at once, but I don't really like doing that. I never know what I will want to say on a particular day!

How personal do you get on your account?

Not as personal as some. I try to create a happy, calming space and keep any personal difficulties away from my account. No judgment to those who do. I'd just rather my own experience on social media be positive, and that wouldn't be possible if I were posting negatively. That said, I want my followers to know me and who I am, so I try to share snippets of my day as regularly as I can.

Chapter 9: FOLLOWING HASHTAGS

Did you know that you can follow hashtags on Instagram as well as people? True story. If you go to the hashtag's feed, either by clicking it on a post or searching for it, you get the option to follow that hashtag. Here are a few ways to use this feature to your advantage.

Follow your own hashtags

Follow your author name, your series names, your books' names. That way, if anyone is talking about your books but they didn't tag you, you're less likely to miss it. So I follow: #hannasandvig #faerietaleromances #therosegate.

It's always a good idea to comment on posts that share your books and share them in your Stories. And if you have a fan who doesn't know you're on Instagram, they might be excited to follow you.

Follow genre specific hashtags

You might need to do a bit of creative digging to find the best hashtags for this. You want something that is used often but is as specific as possible to your genre. I write fairy tale retellings, so I follow—wait for it—#fairytaleretellings (also #fairytaleretelling, those plurals always have a singular hashtag).

I try to comment on as many posts with that hashtag as I can because those are my potential readers! They are reading in my genre and talking about the books they've read. Usually I just comment about how I liked the book in the photo, or a fun one I've read recently, but sometimes I recommend my book.

You need to be careful with this. No one goes on Instagram to be spammed by an over eager author. But if the poster is asking for recommendations, and my book is a perfect match, then I let them know. Super casually.

Seriously, please be cool about this.

Someone might post a photo of *A Curse so Dark and Lonely* and say "I love Beauty and the Beast retellings so much, can anyone recommend another one to me?" And I would comment something like "Oh, I just finished that one, Grey was my favorite character. I actually wrote a Beauty and the Beast retelling! It's called *The Rose Gate*, and it's on Amazon."

I have sold books this way, and no one has gotten annoyed, because I'm engaging in natural conversation and recommending a book they're asking for. If I recommended my book a hundred times a day to anyone who likes YA fantasy, I would have no friends and possibly be blocked for spamming. But if I honestly think my book is a good fit for a reader, I'll let them know about it.

Make a hashtag for a group of friends

My author group has its own hashtag and we all follow it so that we don't miss each other's posts. We can also click on it to see everyone's posts and catch up. Shout out to my fellow #queensofthequill!

INTERVIEW WITH: *Danielle Jensen*

Handle: @danielleljensen
Followers: 8.8k
Account style: Author
Genre: YA Fantasy

How long have you been on Instagram, and where were you in your publishing journey when you started?
I've been on Instagram since 2015, which was about a year after my first novel was published.

Do you feel that Instagram helps you sell books? How else is it helpful to you as an author.

It absolutely helps sell books! I consider Instagram, and bookstagram, integral to my marketing strategy and it is where I focus the majority of my effort. It helps with keeping my readers informed of what I'm up to, as well as provides an informal method of contacting me (DMs).

Do you do anything special for a book launch on Instagram?

Prior to a book launch, I tend to do a lot of posts that attempt to engage with readers. My goal is comments and shares rather than likes.

Which posts get the most engagement for you?

New covers or artwork tend to get the most engagement, but readers also enjoy posts about upcoming releases more than they do posts about books already in the wild. Posts with me in the image also get a lot of engagement, but I'm not a huge fan of being photographed, so those are rare on my feed.

Do you have a strategy for balancing the sort of posts you make?

What I post about is typically determined by news or information that I want to put in front of my readers. It's difficult to plan far in advance because I don't necessarily have control over when certain information is made public. I currently post four photos for every one quote graphic. Instagram tends to favor photos over graphics in its algorithm, but I've found that is a great balance.

What do you take your photos with? Do you use any editing software?

I take my photos with an iPhone and I edit with the phone's software or in Lightroom. I also use Photoshop with stock photo flat lays or backgrounds layered with whatever book I'm featuring.

How do you like to use Stories?

I primarily use Stories to share posts I've been tagged in or to more informally communicate information. Stories and DMs are where a huge portion of my engagement with readers takes place, and I believe people enjoy the one-on-one connection.

How personal do you get on your account?

Not at all. I keep my posts almost entirely related to my novels and writing. I'm a very private person, so I don't share photos of my family or talk about them very often.

My children are too young to give informed consent to having their images shared, so I've made a commitment not to do so on any social media platform.

How much time do you devote to Instagram in a day or week?

I spend about eight hours a week on Instagram, the majority of it responding to direct messages and comments from readers.

Do you have any advice for authors on using Instagram?

I think the key to success with Instagram is engagement. If readers are taking the time to comment on your posts or to send you a message, you should take the time to respond to them. That said, it can become a huge drain on an author's time, so it's important to learn how to step back from social media and focus on the true work, which is writing.

PART 1 - THE BASICS

PART 2: *Connecting With Readers*

Chapter 10: ENGAGEMENT

You'll sometimes hear people say that social media isn't as much about the number of followers as the engagement. I completely believe this. Followers are useless (to you—they are probably still awesome humans) if they aren't engaging with your content. Engagement is the interaction you get on your posts. Comments, likes, shares, saves.

There are two reasons why engagement is important. First, if people are interacting with your posts, you're building relationships with them. And relationships sell books. Secondly, the magical algorithm will show them your posts more often if they engage with you. So you might have five thousand followers, but only the ones that engage with your posts even see them. If Instagram thinks someone isn't interested in your content anymore, they'll move it down their feed and bump up the posts it thinks they'll like. Or maybe if they interact occasionally with your posts, it'll show them half of what you post and three days late.

If you want your followers to keep seeing your content, you need to make posts that people love to interact with.

The first way to increase engagement is by posting interesting photos that make people want to comment and share them in their Stories. This could be because they are really aesthetically pleasing photos, or because the subject is something people love, like a very popular book. Or your cat. Generally, a great image will get you more likes, but people still may not comment, and you want those comments!

The easiest way to encourage people to comment on your posts is to ask a question. It should be about them, not you. And ideally, it should be quick and easy to answer. A lot of people put a question near the bottom of their caption, but I like to put mine right at the beginning. Instagram only shows the first 125 characters of your caption before linking to the rest, so you want the question to be right there where people will see it as they scroll. It should be something to make them stop scrolling because they just have to tell you the answer. But make it simple. If I see a question that makes me think too long, I'll just keep scrolling while I think, and I usually won't go back to answer it.

Here are some examples of questions to ask:

- What are you reading right now, and do you like it?

- What's the last book you finished, and do you recommend it?

- What book are you planning to read next?

- Are you a mood reader, or do you have a TBR (To Be Read list)?

- Do you drink coffee or tea?

- What was your favorite book as a kid?

- Would you ever arrange your bookshelves in rainbow order?

- Do you read e-books or print books?

- Werewolves or vampires?

- If you had a superpower, what would it be?

- What's your favorite genre?

- Who's your favorite fictional couple?

- Are you a cat person or a dog person?

What's the last book that made you stay up past your bedtime?

Get the idea? Tie them into your photo if you can. Always answer your own question in the caption. And then reply to each and every comment that you get. For extra credit, go to each of the commenter's accounts and comment on one of their photos. You might not get to every single commenter, but this is a great practice for strengthening those relationships.

Sometimes the questions get old or you just can't think of one. Games to the rescue! Here are some examples of games you can play in your captions:

Predictive text

This uses the predictive text function on a mobile device. You know, those words that appear as you're typing when your phone tries to guess what you're going to say next? You give the beginning of a sentence in the caption, and they choose words from the predictive text to answer. And then you laugh together at the result. Such as:

I'm writing a story about _____ (and predictive text fills in the blank)

Or one with a couple blanks like:

I went to the _____ and I saw _____

Just don't make these too long, or people will forget half of it and have to scroll up to reread it, and then you've lost most of them. For a cover reveal, it can be fun to remove words from the book's title and see what the predictive text fills in.

Battery percentage

The idea of this game is to pick a few options and assign them to battery percentages left on your phone. Then your followers look at their phone's charge and reply with which option they've gotten. Such as:

80-100% - Vampire

60-80% - Faerie

40-60% - Wizard

20-40% - Werepoodle

1-20% - Surly weasel

I'm currently at 83% and therefore a vampire.

This or That

At its simplest, this is a choice between two things:

Chocolate or butterscotch?

Don't trust anyone who answers butterscotch.

Or you can pick a theme and do 3-5 this or that questions:

Beach or Pool?

Popsicle or Ice cream?

Romcom or Thriller?

Barefoot or Flipflops?

And then they'll comment, saying: Beach, Ice cream, Romcom, Barefoot! Or at least, that's what I would pick. I like to keep it light, but feel free to do murder clowns or chainsaw killers if that's more your style.

Fill in the Blanks

This is similar to predictive text, but you give them a criteria for the blank words. Such as:

Queen/King (the color of your shirt) of (the last thing you ate).

Making me Queen Turquoise of Spinach.

There are more games out there, just watch people's captions or do a google search. Always give your own answer (it builds—wait for it—relationships!) and you can chatter a bit after to round out the caption.

INTERVIEW WITH: *Samantha*

Handle: @everlasting.charm
Followers: 120k
Account style: Bookstagram (influencer)

When did you start your account?
I started my account in August of 2015.

Which posts get the most engagement for you?
I find that bookshelf photos do really well, but also photos of my bedroom. Wide view pictures of my whole room do better than pictures of corners of my bedroom.

What's your favorite thing about the community?

I've found bookstagram to be like a sibling. It can be annoying and drama filled, but when push comes to shove, they are there for you and so supportive.

What do you take your photos with? Do you use any editing software?

I use my iPhone 11 max. I also use Snapseed to edit my pictures and VSCO to add a filter.

Do you take your photos in batches, or do you take them and post them immediately?

I used to take pictures well in advance, especially if I knew I wasn't going to be home. Now though I'm trying to be more spontaneous so I take a picture the day I post it.

What are a couple of caption types or questions that you like best?

I know this varies person to person so, personally, I prefer short captions. More than half the time, I don't read captions. I'm there for the pictures. So I do like generic questions like: what are you reading? What are you watching? Also, this-or-that questions are my fave!

Do you do promo posts on your feed? Traditional only, or indie as well?

I often feature the books publishers send me, but promos of other products are rare.

How do you choose if you're going to promote a book?

The genre. And if it's a book I would actually read. You'll notice I don't promote children or middle grade books because I don't read them. I like to promote books I know I'll truly enjoy and can express that enjoyment to my audience.

Do you have any advice for authors on how to approach influencers?

If there's an email in their bio, use it. Do not send a DM. For me, DMs get lost in the mix or accidentally deleted. It's safer to send an email.

Do you have any tips for authors in creating a cohesive theme?

Filters. Even if you don't have an actual theme, having the same filter for every post will make posts look cohesive. Though I have been reading that trends are changing and no one wants to see filters/theme. So go with your gut and be yourself!

I mentioned back in Chapter 2 that you can choose in your account settings between having a personal account or a professional account. Anyone can set up a professional account. The only real differences are that professional accounts must be public, and the account holder gets access to insights and can promote posts.

To set up your professional account, you'll need to link it to a Facebook page. If you don't have a page for your author business, go ahead and make one. You don't have to post any content on it for Instagram to accept it.

Then choose between a Business account or a Creator account. Business accounts were designed for companies and brands, Creator accounts were designed for individual artists and influencers. A Business account gives you the ability to schedule posts through a service like Hoot-

Suite. A Creator account gives you more detailed data on your followers and posts, and a bit more control over your profile.

I resisted switching from my personal account for a long time, for fear that Instagram would limit the reach of professional accounts the way Facebook has with pages, but I finally took the plunge and I haven't noticed any difference in reach. Instagram appears to limit everyone's reach equally. So you might as well get the insights.

Okay, what are insights? They're the data on how well your posts are doing and who your audience is. You can access insights in two ways.

On a post:

Directly under your photo, there will be a little link that says "view insights." Tap it to see how that post is performing. Now you should be able to see:

- How many likes, comments, shares, and saves the post has received, and if anyone has followed you from that post.

- Profile visits and Reach: This is how many people saw the post. Try not to get depressed when comparing it to your follower count!

- Interactions: profile visits (again), website clicks, and if anyone emailed or called you—if you have those options enabled.

- Discovery: First you see your reach again, and what percent were already following you. I find this interesting because for me, it's usually around 50%, but occasionally I have a post that does very well and it will always have a much higher percentage of accounts who weren't following me. That means the algorithm has decided the post is interesting and it's ranking higher in the hashtag pages.

Then it shows you how many people followed you based on that post, and where the post's viewers came from (Home, Profile, Hashtags, Other). This is a very helpful way to see if you're choosing effective hashtags.

In your profile:

Go to the menu in your profile and choose Insights to view data for your whole feed for a more zoomed-out view of things.

For short term data, choose Highlights. It includes:

- Accounts reached, which shows your activity for the week and your top posts, Stories, and videos.

- Content Interactions is similar but shows it based on likes, comments, saves, and shares.

- Audience shows you cool things like the age, gender, and locations of your audience for the past week, as well as their more active times on Instagram.

Then, if you scroll down to "Content You Shared," you can find some really cool long term data. Click on posts, Stories, or IGTV videos and you can sort them based on a number of variables over different time periods. You can see which posts get the most likes versus which ones got the most comments in the past year, month, or week. I find this super interesting, and it doesn't just show which posts are better—it shows which posts are more likely to get your audience to take different actions (comment, share it in Stories, go to your website, or just like it because it's pretty).

If you don't pay any attention to your data, you might not realize which posts are performing better and why. You might find that you're posting at the wrong time of day, or that some of your hashtags are more effective than others. It can be really helpful to take a look occasionally, then try to do more of the things that are proving to work for you!

Pro tip:

Many accounts can't see other people's likes anymore on the Instagram app. It seems to be location specific (I'm in Canada, and I can't). This is too bad because it's a good way to see what sort of posts are performing well for others. However, they never got rid of likes on the website version. So if you're in the mood to do some research on other author's feeds, open them up on your computer instead of your phone.

Creator Studio

You can post directly from your computer to Instagram if you have a professional account by using Creator Studio. You can currently find it at: business.Facebook .com/creatorstudio. This is a dashboard for your Facebook pages and any Instagram accounts that are connected to those pages. So I can use it to post to my author, illustration, and photography accounts, all from one dashboard. I love using Creator Studio to post because I edit my photos on my computer, so it saves me the step of emailing them to my phone. I also find it easier to copy/paste hashtags from other posts and my notepad hashtag document.

I do find that every now and then it glitches while posting and then I have to start over, so I always copy my carefully crafted caption before posting. A good idea, no matter what app you post with, as it can be incredibly frustrating to rewrite your whole caption.

INTERVIEW WITH: *James Fahy*

Handle: @jamesfahyauthor
Followers: 31k
Account style: Author
Genre: Urban Gothic

How long have you been on Instagram, and where were you in your publishing journey when you started?

I've been on Insta since 2015, ever since my Agent landed me my first publishing deal for my debut novel *Isle of Winds*, and both the publishers and my agency insisted it was productive for me to have an "online presence." It's definitely changed a lot as a platform from back then. People, even those within the book-loving community, use it very differently now than they did when I joined. I still enjoy it greatly, though, or I wouldn't still be here.

Do you feel that Instagram helps you sell books? How else is it helpful to you as an author?

Oh, there's absolutely no question that having active social media platforms leads to higher book sales, whether that's Facebook, Twitter, or Instagram. At the most basic level, it increases your visibility, and you're tapping into a huge community (or rather many overlapping communities) of book lovers and enthusiasts. Long gone are the days when authors were mysterious and nebulous presences, far out of the reach of people. Readers like authors to be accessible, and they like to be able to interact with them. As an author, I enjoy interacting with my readers just as much.

Which posts get the most engagement for you?

It's not something I've ever really tracked. I'm more the post-and-go mentality. If something occurs to me that I want to share, whether that's about my writing, my books, or something completely remote from my career, I don't really worry about what engagement or impact it has. I've never fussed over a post worrying why it has less likes than a previous post; or patted myself on the back for a post getting higher likes than average. I'm here to have conversations and connections with people, not to score dopamine points from a list of electronic heart emojis.

Do you have a strategy for balancing the sort of posts you make?

Absolutely not. I've referred to my feed before now as a "casserole of nonsense," and I mean that quite affectionately. I get incredibly bored if I look at someone's feed on Insta and it's rigid and regimented. "Monday we post this, Tuesday it's cats, Wednesday it's a book teaser, weekends it's self-promotion" etc. That bores the socks off me and it never feels spontaneous or genuine. I guess the only thing I consciously do is try not to post too much of the same thing in a row.

Some people follow my feed for book-talk, others follow it for landscape pics, some poor creatures for my surreal selfies, so it all works out. My only regular scheduled thing is the weekends, where I tend to pop a post linking to my blog on my website, where I update weekly. Other than that, it's anyone's guess what I might post next.

What do you take your photos with? Do you use any editing software?

I take 100% of my pictures with my iPhone. It's small, it's handy, it has a decent camera and gets the job done. I don't do a huge amount of editing on posts that are about books, or landscape or nature posts, or posts about food. Generally, for those I will just tinker with Insta's own internal filters, etc.

The one thing I do use a lot are animation and special effects filters when I make posts that have my face in them, because I generally think regular selfies can be extremely boring. I will occasionally post the odd "normal" picture, if I have something not light-hearted to talk about. But at least 90% of selfies that I do post I try to make dumb or silly or at least visually entertaining, and I usually end up with animated flames, or inserted backgrounds, or strange art filters over my face making me a demon or a merman or something else odd. Photolab, Werble, Frames and Snow are all fun apps to play around with for photo manipulation.

Do you take your photos in batches, or do you take them and post them immediately?

I've never taken photos in batches. I don't usually take a picture until something occurs to me that I want to share online. If I have a book I've finished, or something is happening in my little writer's world, or I see a particularly nice sunset, anything I decide I want to share, I'll usually snap a pic there and then, and upload it the same day. I like the immediacy of that.

I think if I ever took a week's worth of photos and meticulously planned out what I was going to post each day and when, it would absolutely suck out the fun and spontaneity of what I enjoy about social media. It would just become a list of chores for me. I'd rather be as in-the-dark as my followers are about what kind of things I'm going to post next.

How personal do you get on your account?

There's definitely a balance to be struck. My social media platforms are very informal and quite light-hearted (I take my job seriously, but very little else in life). But at the end of the day, they're still work accounts. They still represent me professionally, so while I like to think that I'm quite open and I try to give as much of myself to people as I can and remain genuine, there are unspoken lines I don't cross.

I only share maybe 10% of what's going on with me online, because much of my life outside of writing involves and affects other people in my family, not just me. I might well be perfectly comfortable having my face and my thoughts splashed all over the internet, but I've no right to assume that's the same for my partner or kids.

How much time do you devote to Instagram in a day or week?

Much less than I used to. I think social media can be a bit of a black hole you fall into, and it can eat up your time and sap your productivity.

I know people in the author community on Insta who genuinely worry about things like engagement, and panic if they don't strictly post something absolutely every day for fear of losing followers, or getting lost in the noise. It can become their master, not their servant. But I will only post something if I have something to post or say, not just for the sake of "keeping up." I think it's important to remember that social media is a tool (a fun one), not an obligation.

My healthy balance these days is that I will generally scroll through Insta and Twitter first thing in the morning while I'm having my first coffee, then I don't look at it again until lunch, when (if I have anything to post) I'll pop it on and see what everyone at my Insta-table is up to in their lives. Then usually the phone goes away until evening, as I have writing to be getting on with and don't need the distraction.

Any other tips for authors who want to get started with Instagram?

I can only really say what works for me, and that's to try and be genuine, try to be varied, don't be preachy or pompous, be approachable, but don't offer up your entire personal life to the internet. Focus on building good and rewarding connections with creatives rather than obsessing over followers and likes, and for the love-...of...all...that's...holy, don't spam your feed with nothing but your own books. That just makes your profile and your feed feel like a hard-sell rolling infomercial, and it will discourage people from wanting to interact with you.

Social media isn't a cold-call to hawk your products. It's a genuine opportunity to interact with book lovers and with your readers, to a scale that writers in earlier times simply didn't have the opportunity to enjoy. If people believe you're genuine and not just pushing a product as though you were a marketing department, it's been my experience that they're far more likely to be intrigued to see what your writing is like, once they've gotten to know the person behind it.

Chapter 12 : SELLING BOOKS

You could have tens of thousands of followers and feel super famous, but that's not really the point of Instagram for an author, is it? We don't just want high numbers, we want to make connections with readers who will be interested in our books. Even if you're still writing your very first manuscript, you'll want to create an audience that's excited to buy your book. This means you need to be sure to tell them about your books. Sounds simple? It is, but many of us get all twitchy when we need to "sell."

I try to remember that I actually really like my stories. I think they're great. Other people like them, too. So really, it's doing my audience a favor to let them know about this story that they might enjoy reading. If you don't believe your story is worth selling, you need to take a long hard look at your books and your self confidence. We aren't trying to scam people or sell them something they won't like. You're trying to sell a book to people who like books. You've hopefully started attracting readers who will enjoy a book just like yours, so don't hide it from them!

When you're selling in a post, it's even more important to use the engagement strategies we've discussed. Have a great photo. Ask a question in your caption. Use all the hashtags. These will boost the visibility of your post.

I split talking about my books into two categories: Hard Sells and Soft Sells.

Soft Sells

To me, a soft sell is me casually mentioning my book. This book exists (or will exist). This is what my book's about. Here's a cool character from my book. Soft sells are photos of your workspace with an explanation of your WIP, posting character art, squealing over how happy you are to have gotten a stack of your author copies in the mail. A soft sell is a reminder that you are an author, and that you have a book.

Hard Sells

A hard sell, to me, is when I say "I wrote this book, it's available here...you'll love it." A hard sell could include a reader review, a sale promotion, a cover reveal with a pre-order announcement.

The longer I'm on Instagram, and the further I am in my author career, the easier time I have with the hard sell. I've realized that when I talk about the same book more than once, I might sound like a broken record to myself, but I don't to my followers.

Not all your followers see every post, and if they do, they might not read every caption. Between the way people scroll without clicking on the "read more" link and the way the algorithm mixes posts around, you should assume that it will take more than one post for even an engaged fan to notice something. And your really engaged fans won't mind hearing about your books over and over. In fact, you can ask them to share your selling posts in their Stories, and some will do it without being asked.

I've had people follow me for months before clueing in that I'm an author, and I post about my books twice a week on average.

That said, both the hard and soft sell have their place. Mix them up, and share things that seem fun and genuine. Both these strategies have sold my books and added subscribers to my newsletter.

Because Instagram will only be useful for selling books if you actually sell your books there.

INTERVIEW WITH: *Becky Moynihan*

Handle: @becky_moynihan
Followers: 1.4k
Account style: Author
Genre: YA Dystopian/NA Urban Fantasy

How long have you been on Instagram, and where were you in your publishing journey when you started?
I've had a personal Instagram account for many years, maybe a decade or so, but it was private and I used it like Facebook. In 2017, when I started writing my debut novel, I discovered the power of hashtags, which then took me on a social media journey I didn't expect. Soon after, I found the incredible bookstagram community!

You have a dedicated Instagram street team. How did you start it, and how does it work for you?

Shortly before releasing my second novel, I started noticing how several indie authors were utilizing street teams and ARC teams. But most were set up on FB as group pages, yet my reader following was mostly on Instagram, so I decided to set up a "group page" on Instagram. I simply announced in my Stories and on a post one day that I was looking to set up a street/ARC team, and anyone who'd read my books could join. After a quick poll, I discovered that most preferred group chat over email, so I set up one big DM group called "Elite Bananas." Ahem, there's a story behind that name and the group wasn't originally called that (Becky's Elite Book Warriors was the original). As the group bonded though, a name change was inevitable.

At first, I tried keeping comments to a minimum, fearing the members would get annoyed at all the messages. That didn't last long though. The more we chatted, the closer we became—and the more dedicated my team was to reading and promoting my books! They are the first to receive teasers of my WIPs (works in progress), and first to see new covers and swag art. They also receive digital copies of my books a few weeks before release day. In return, they review my books and share sales, cover reveals, and new releases on their social media accounts. It's a win-win! I absolutely adore my Instagram street team and am so glad I decided to give it a go even though I really didn't know what to expect.

Do you feel that Instagram helps you sell books? How else is it helpful to you as an author?

Yes, it helps. Maybe not in a "make a living off my book sales" way, but it helps strengthen my readership foundation. I most actively communicate with my fans on Instagram, and my efforts to build relationships with them result in dedicated readers who genuinely want to share my books with their friends and family. That word of mouth credibility is invaluable!

Do you do anything special for a book launch on Instagram?

I always do at least one of these things: mark a pre-existing book on sale, share countdown teasers, do a giveaway, or host a live Q&A. Beyond that, I rally my street team and dedicated readers/followers to share share share the new release!

What's a mistake you see authors making on Instagram?

Not engaging with their readers. Unless you're a super popular author with a large readership, posting a quick "Buy my book!" probably won't glean the results you're hoping for. You're more than a book. You're a person with a life story to tell, so be genuine and let your readers know that you're real and reachable! Another mistake is only socializing with fellow writers/authors. They hold great value in your personal and business life, don't get me wrong, but readers usually hold more credibility when they share their book recommendations!

Do you have any advice for authors on using Instagram?

Figure out what exactly you want out of the platform. A large following? Well posting dozens of "buy my book" graphics won't gain you an audience. Study what the bookstagrammers are posting, readers and authors alike. Engagement is key, but posting eye-catching, relevant content is a must. Also, a large following doesn't guarantee you readers and book sales. It's important to find your audience. If you write horror, engaging with a bunch of contemporary romance readers probably won't help you. Another important thing to note is that not all readers read self-published books. Some strictly stick with the mainstream popular traditionally published books, which means you'll have to do some digging to find the indie readers out there if you're an indie author. But don't worry, there's lots of them! You simply have to find them.

Which posts get the most engagement for you?

The ones where I ask a relatable question, cover reveals, and any other "new" thing, like new series announcements, title reveals, or bookish swag reveals. During the lulls when I don't have something new and exciting to show, posting pretty book pics with a relatable question keeps the engagement going!

What's your favorite thing about the community?

The pride and care readers show in their gorgeous bookish photos, and the genuine enthusiasm to bond with people who love books.

How personal do you get on your account?

I talk about my personal life when something interesting and relatable is happening, but I try to keep the topics positive in nature. There's plenty I could complain and rant about, but that's a great way to alienate people. I'm not saying everything has to be sunshine and rainbows, but when you start sneaking in touchy subjects like politics, you can bet that some people will flee for the hills. If that's not a worry of yours, then post away!

Chapter 13: BUILDING COMMUNITY

My favorite thing about Instagram is the friends I've made there, both with readers and other authors. That sounds cheesy, but it's true. Let's chat about the author community first.

One day on Facebook (am I allowed to talk about Facebook in this book? I promise it's just for a minute) in a big author group, someone posted a thread asking if anyone wanted to be in an Instagram comment pod (more on comment pods in Chapter 15). The idea was that we would all like and comment on each other's posts to try and boost our posts up a bit in the algorithm.

So, we did. We got to know each other through our regular posts and did what we could to promote each other's books.

Later on, that group combined with another author pod (I think they were both Kay L Moody's fault) and we formed a Facebook group with the most active members to chat about author stuff. That group has now evolved into Queens of the Quill, a mastermind group with twelve engaged members, a Slack chat, a weekly zoom meeting, and soon a podcast. Eight of us have an anthology together as a result of our joint write-to-market exercises.

We help each other with blurbs, pimp each other's books, and generally support each other. I love these ladies, and I don't know what I'd do without them. And I owe it all to the relationships we started on Instagram.

I also got plugged into a great author community, met my editor, gained illustration clients, and have had chats with authors well above my level, just by interacting and being friendly.

In real life, I'm an introvert. It's sometimes easier online. What have you got to lose?

So how do you meet these authors? Like I did, you can find threads on Facebook, if you're already plugged in there. Or start one yourself.

You can search author related hashtags like #amwriting, #indieauthorsunite, or #indieauthorsofInstagram. You can also search for monthly photo challenges for authors, or just start looking for your favorite authors and follow them!

Just be friendly, comment on people's posts and Stories. Be genuine and you'll be able to make real connections over time.

Making reader connections is, of course, very valuable as well.

I view Instagram as one of the few places where I can interact with readers at the beginning of the buyer's journey. Top of the funnel. Cold. Whatever they are in marketing jargon. What I'm trying to say is, Instagram can introduce people who have never heard of your books to you and they can slowly (or quickly) evolve into your readers, and from there to your superfans. Because people are already on Instagram as part of the bookstagram community to learn about books, it's a ready-made audience. Many readers find all their books based on the recommendations from bookstagrammers.

That's the power of the bookstagram community. By interacting with bookish accounts and posting about your book in your feed, you'll become a part of this community and help people become aware of you and your Stories. You can make followers, fans and even friends who want to read your next book, join your newsletter, and help you promote your next new release.

I've seen more than one new author launch a debut novel with a lot of buzz and support, simply because they've made connections with people who will help them.

Personally, I was able to get beta readers, newsletter subscribers, and pre-orders for my debut novel just through Instagram. If it wasn't for that community, I'm certain that I would have launched to crickets. And I continue to make sales through my Instagram posts eighteen months later.

If you plan to publish through a traditional publisher, an engaged community following your Instagram account can make you much more attractive to agents. They get a lot of great manuscripts, and every advantage you can get will help you get published.

INTERVIEW WITH: *C.M. Karys*

(Coauthors Chiara and Maria)

Handles: @_ckarys @_mkarys
Followers: 18.2k and 14.3k
Account styles: Bookstagram
Genre: NA Fantasy

How long have you ladies been on Instagram, and where were you in your publishing journey when you started?

Chiara joined Instagram in November 2016, while Maria joined March 2017. At that time, publishing was a distant dream. We both knew we wanted to use our platform as a way to talk about our writing and build an audience for our books, but we hadn't found the right story to try to pursue publishing just yet. *Ilahara: The Last Myrassar,* the book we are going to be publishing next year, was born shortly after we joined the community, and from the first moment, we knew that story would be different. So building our bookstagram accounts and finding the right story to tell came hand in hand.

Your debut novel, Ilahara: The Last Myrasser is coming out through Literary Wanderlust. Do you think your social media platform was helpful in being picked up?

Absolutely! Social media presence is really important in the publishing business nowadays, especially when pursuing self-publishing or indie publishing. That's not to say your book will immediately be picked up if you have a large audience, because we've gotten some rejections along the way before signing with Literary Wanderlust, but it definitely helps to bring more awareness to your book and to build a relationship with your future readers.

You've commissioned quite a bit of artwork for your book. Do you think this has helped build interest in the story?

It definitely has. Something we realized by being in the book community is that many readers (us included) love artwork, and are more likely to enjoy a special edition book or a book box if there is artwork by a fan-favorite artist included. That's why we reached out to Gabriella Bujdoso for our commissions. Not only is she a great friend and our favorite artist, but she's also very beloved in the community and her support helped us attract more attention to *Ilahara*.

How personal do you get on your accounts?

We both try to get as personal as possible on our accounts. We won't share every single detail of our lives to keep a degree of privacy for our family, but we both love to share fun facts about our days, especially in regards to our writing process and inspiration. Or our dog. Unfortunately we can't feature her often because she's camera shy.

What sort of posts get the most engagement for you?

It really depends on the days and on the algorithm's mood. Popular books definitely attract more likes, but posts about *Ilahara* get more comments. We also notice that flat lay setups tend to receive more love than angled shots, unless it's a shelfie!

How much time do you devote to Instagram in a day or week?

The average time we spend on Instagram is anywhere from 4-6 hours a day, depending on how busy we are. Most of that time goes into interacting with our friends and followers in DMs and in the comments section. The time we have to be online definitely drops when we're deep into the editing cave, as we like to call it. We try to be more engaging when it's time for the writing cave.

How do you support each other and other accounts on Instagram?

It's important to be engaging with the community. Between us, we share each other's post each night to broaden our reach. When we can, we also like to share posts that we particularly like from that day in our Stories. Along with some friends (@tata.lifepages, @ve_xo, @giota_the_reader, @drawingandreading, @kimcarlika, @shaked_reads, @pretty_little_library, @asthebookends, @darkest.night.sky, @queenof_midnight, @booksbreathemagic) we also created a hashtag called #inspiredbybookish, where each week we choose one picture for everyone joining the challenge to recreate in their own style, giving proper credit to the original creator.

Our favorite shots receive a shout-out in our Stories. We also like to host shout-out sessions, which we find to be a good way to discover new accounts and reach new bookstagrammers while also helping others in return. It's also important to engage with mutual followers with likes and comments. We try to return the love to as many people as we can each day.

What are a couple of caption types or questions that you like best?

Our captions have a pretty standard structure: we share something about our day, a reading update or our thoughts on the book we're featuring; next, we leave a question for our followers to reply to in comments. Some of our favorites to do are predictive text games or battery percentage games, which are quick and fun at the same time.

How do you use Stories?

We use Stories mostly to give our followers a glimpse into our lives and create a more "human" connection that goes beyond the post. We like showing our faces in Stories and talking "face to face" with our audience. Be it an unboxing or a book haul or even a behind the scenes into photos or writing, they're a fun way to connect.

What's your favorite thing about the bookstagram community?

Apart from the possibility to discover new books and engage with people with similar interests, the best part about the community is the possibility to build lasting friendships. Some of our mutual followers have become our closest friends over the years, and that's something we cherish.

Do you have any advice for aspiring authors on using Instagram?

Our best advice would be to spend time curating your page. It's not enough to post a picture of a computer screen or a desk or a graphic with your book's cover and title. Instagram is a visual platform, and you're more likely to succeed if you have a cohesive aesthetic to your content. It's also a good idea not to limit yourself to your writing. The more elements you give people to connect with you, the more likely you are to create a lasting community around you.

Chapter 14: PHOTO CHALLENGES

A great way to get involved in both the booksta-gram community and the Instagram author community is with monthly photo challenges.

Every month, organizers will post a challenge graphic with prompts. Usually daily prompts, sometimes weekly. The idea is that you post a photo that ties in to the day's prompt, and use the challenge's hashtag in your caption.

Most organizers don't expect you to participate in every prompt for the month. It's more of a "join in when you can" sort of thing.

I usually participate in five to ten challenges every month.

I hear you screaming internally. It's not as crazy as it sounds, I promise. Here's how I manage it.

First, I save the posts with the monthly challenges. People usually post a graphic with the challenge near the end of the month, and when I come across one, I save it. You can create folders in the "saved" section of your account, and I keep a folder just for challenges. At the beginning of the month, I go through that folder and see which challenges look fun. One might be a really good fit, so I might mentally commit to doing as many as I can for that one. Sometimes (because I take photos in advance), I might plan photos for a date that showcases books that fit the prompt really well. It depends on how organized I want to be.

Lately, though, because I've got other criteria for my post planning (how often I show my own books, my theme's aesthetic, cover reveals I offered to help with, etc.) I'll often just take the photos I want to take. Then, when I go to post, I'll see how many challenges my photo legitimately works for. It's usually two or three of the ten. Sometimes more, sometimes zero. For each challenge that works with the photo, I'll post the hashtag under my caption with the prompt and maybe a note about why it fits. You can do this however you want, but for me, it looks like this:

#febbookchallenge2020 {enemies to lovers} Cardan and Jude are my favorites!

So why bother? The challenge hashtags give you a visibility boost. Other participants in a challenge will often check the hashtag page and see what other people are posting. And the challenge organizers (who may have a much bigger audience than you) will often do shoutouts in their Stories featuring their favorite photos in their challenges.

It's also just a great way to get to know people, by taking part in a community activity together. You might even have fun! And if you're always searching for ideas of what to post, it's a great way to jumpstart your creativity.

How do you find challenges? First, pay attention to challenge mentions in people's posts. You might find them at the end of the month when any organizers you follow post their challenges for the next month. You can also use hashtags. Try searching for things like: #bookstagramchallenge #bookishchallenge #authorchallenge

There are accounts that repost as many challenges as they can find, like @challengesofbookstagram. There is even a very cool website by Kell Jasmer that helps you find challenges and organize the ones you want to participate in. All you have to do is select the ones that look interesting from her monthly selection (I think she tries to find as many as she can) and it creates a daily list of the hashtags and prompts for each challenge that day. Find it at https://kelljasmer.com/challenges.

I don't know a shortcut for finding monthly author community challenges, but if you follow fellow authors and keep your eyes peeled, you'll find them.

Monthly challenges are a great way to get to know the bookstagram community. You might like them so much you start to organize your own!

INTERVIEW WITH: *Kandi Steiner*

Handle: @kandisteiner
Followers: 24.8k
Account style: Author
Genre: Contemporary Romance

How long have you been on Instagram, and where were you in your publishing journey when you started?
I've been on Instagram since 2011. I was still a student at the University of Central Florida at the time. I started writing my first romance novel in 2012, and published it in 2013.

Do you feel that Instagram helps you sell books? How else is it helpful to you as an author.

Absolutely! But, to me, Instagram is more about being in the book community. I love to talk about books, see the creative edits and photography that bloggers, authors, and readers alike capture. It just feels like hanging out with all my book buddies. But yes, Instagram is very helpful to an author's brand, especially if they consider that you shouldn't be trying to sell anything directly. It's all about being yourself, being in the community, and raising awareness about your books.

Do you do anything special for a book launch on Instagram?

I usually post on my feed, Stories, maybe a reel, and will run an ad or two. I always do an after release day giveaway, and leading up to release, I'll post teasers and countdowns.

Do you have any advice for authors on using Instagram?

Just be yourself! Don't focus on trying to sell something. Focus on creating content that you love.

Which posts get the most engagement for you?

Usually the pictures of me and my boyfriend, or me traveling, LOL.

Do you have a strategy for balancing the sort of posts you make?
Kind of! I have what I call my "pillars." So, there's writing, my books, books I love, travel, Florida life, my cat, and my personal life.

What do you take your photos with? Do you use any editing software?
I use an iPhone 11 Pro and LightRoom.

Do you take your photos in batches, or do you take them and post them immediately?
It depends! A little of both.

How personal do you get on your account?
Very. My followers are like my BFFs.

How much time do you devote to Instagram in a day or week?
I don't track it. I guess if you consider the time it takes to take the photos, edit them, write captions and hashtags,

post Stories, and engage with comments/messages, probably 1-3 hours a day depending on if it's a busy day.

Sometimes social media seems unfair. The people who have a big following get all the algorithm love, but how do you get a following when no one sees your posts? Instagrammers have come up with a few ways to try and help each other get more visibility. The idea is to get enough comments/likes/shares/saves to make the algorithm think that you are one of the popular kids and give you more visibility. This will boost you higher in people's feeds, and it will boost you higher on the hashtag pages, making it more likely that new people will follow you.

But is it worth it?

The trouble is, while these tactics can work, they aren't actually short cuts. They take daily time and attention. If you want to make Instagram your number one marketing channel, it could be worth it. Even doing it for a month to get a boost in followers might be worth it.

Only you can decide if the extra time and attention is worth it.

But if you wanted insider secrets, here they are.

Comment Pods

Comment Pods are super simple. The idea is to get a handful of authors together and comment on each other's posts. Getting comments soon after posting is great social proof, and it makes you look better to the mysterious Instagram algorithm.

I spent a while in a pod of authors that my friend Kay L Moody put together. (We weren't friends at the time. This is yet another way to meet other authors and build community!) Our pod was organized in a group chat. When someone had a new post, they put a camera emoji in the chat. Then the rest of the group members saw it and left a comment on the post. When we were done commenting, we "hearted" the camera in the group chat to show that we did it.

The expectation with this sort of group is that people in the pod will comment on everyone's posts, or have a reason why they aren't (on holidays, broke both arms, forgot to pay their internet bill). It's not great to have uncommitted people posting and not helping everyone else in return.

It's very helpful, if you are asking for comments in a pod, to make your post easy to leave a comment on. Same as any post, ask easy questions, play a game, make it about the commenter. Your podmates are doing you a favor, be nice to them.

Result:

I think that this could work if you have a big enough group and they all commented within 24 hours. Our group was small with varying engagement, and I don't think that it really moved the engagement needle all that much. If you are posting to crickets, this could be a good way to have comments on your posts, making it more inviting for other people to join the conversation. Currently, my author group has a hashtag instead and it's more casual, but still a nice way to make sure we don't miss each other's posts.

Engagement Groups

Engagement groups are basically a way of getting likes for likes. The group admins will set up a new private Instagram account and invite interested people to follow it. Then every time a group member posts, they tag the group account in the post. All the posts show up on the group account's "tagged" page and the members are expected to like (and save in some groups) each post. The groups tend to have 200 members. So each time you post, presumably, 199 people will like it. And then you have to like the posts of 199 people every day (and some people post two or three times a day).

As I write this, I am in two large groups and one smaller one. Can you do the math? It's taking me at least half an hour a day just to keep up. If you don't keep up, you'll likely end up kicked out of the group because these groups only work if everyone contributes. And you probably won't be able to join a group like this unless you're a very active Instagrammer who posts daily or close to.

Result:

You can't trust your likes as a way to track engagement if you do this, but my follower count is increasing at about triple the speed it used to (I currently average about 6 followers a day) and I've made some good relationships with people I've met in the groups. The groups I'm in are bookstagram specific. I'm not sure I want to keep it up forever. I mean, half an hour a day on top of my regular Instagram time is a lot.

The moral of the story? Yes, you can get ahead faster with engagement groups. But only you can decide if it's worth your time. There's also the risk that Instagram will decide certain practices count as spam. You especially need to watch liking a lot of posts in a short amount of time, which can get you temporarily thrown in "Instagram jail," meaning you won't be able to post or interact for a bit. It's not permanent, but it's annoying.

INTERVIEW WITH: *Kay L Moody*

Handle: @kaylmoody
Followers: 2.4k
Account style: Bookstagram (author)
Genre: YA fantasy

How long have you been on Instagram, and where were you in your publishing journey when you started?
I started my author Instagram account 2.5 years ago. I started my account 3 months before I published my first book.

I know that you've worked with other authors on a few strategies for building engagement around your Instagram account. Could you tell us a bit about what you've tried? What's worked, and what wasn't worth the effort?

The first thing I did with other authors was to create an Instagram "pod." I actually started with three groups, but several people didn't participate so those three quickly became two groups. Those groups were really strong for over a year.

Eventually, the Instagram algorithm kind of "recognized" that we were all friends. We didn't get a boost in engagement anymore just by commenting on each other's photos because Instagram expected us to. Hopefully that makes sense. But having comments from each other was still helpful because it encouraged comments from our other followers. I think a lot of readers are nervous to be the first person to comment on an author's photo. But if they see a bunch of comments from other people, they'll be more willing to comment. Overall, those pods increased my engagement more than anything else I've ever tried.

After a while, these pods became even more helpful. We started doing newsletter swaps for each other whenever we had new releases. Eventually, our Instagram chat got crowded with the newsletter swap discussions. So, we started a Facebook group. Once we had a Facebook group, we started getting help with blurbs, book covers, marketing questions, etc. That group has become incredibly helpful to all of us! We are a pretty tight knit group of friends now.

I have used another method to increase engagement on Instagram that also works pretty well. I find an author who writes books really similar to mine. Then, I'll check out their most recent posts, specifically the comments. I click on the username of someone who has commented on the photo and then I'll go and leave a comment on THAT person's most recent post. Then I go back to the original post and click on another username of someone who has commented. I continue until I've commented on at least 4-5 people's photos. This is a great way to find readers who are already reading books similar to mine. I've found a lot of really awesome readers with this method.

Do you feel that Instagram helps you sell books? How else is it helpful to you as an author?

I do think it has helped me sell books, but it's kind of tricky to keep track of the sales that actually come from Instagram. What has worked for me is talking about my books a lot. My followers will interact with those posts, but they aren't really interested in buying my book right away. It's not until they've seen several posts about my book that they finally decide to buy it. But by then, they are already very familiar with the title and my name, so they don't go through the link in my bio. They just head straight to their retailer of choice.

Another thing that helps me is having bookstagram-friendly book covers. I have typography covers as opposed to covers that feature a person. These covers tend to do better on Instagram, which makes people more likely to stop scrolling to check it out.

Do you do anything special for a book launch on Instagram?

On launch day, I like to post an image of me holding my book. I don't post many pictures of myself, so those pictures really stand out in my feed. I also announce that it's launch day and how excited I am about the launch. Those posts always get really great engagement.

I also try to talk about my book for several weeks (and even months) leading up to launch. I might talk about the characters, setting, the magic system, etc. I just mention those things in random posts, even if the image isn't of my book.

After launch is when I put the most focus into talking about my book. I usually post about my book more often in the weeks right after launch. I'll post about that book every 3-5 posts. Again, I talk about the characters, setting, magic system, etc. If I have any illustrations/map that go with the book, I'll share those images too.

In my mind, it's not about pushing people to read my book. It's more about reminding them my book exists and informing them about the experience they will have by reading it.

Do you have any advice for authors on using Instagram?
My biggest advice is to create a caption that increases engagement. For me, I always start every single caption with a question. These are fun questions that my followers are excited to answer. This is a great way to get to know my followers. Plus it's fun to see their answers!

What's your favorite thing about the community?
I love how excited people get about books! It's so fun to regularly interact with people who love books as much as I do. The readers on Instagram are dying to talk about their favorite books. They love finding people who have

the same favorites as them. It's a great place to gush about the books I love.

What do you take your photos with? Do you use any editing software?

I use my cell phone camera to take my photos. It's a Samsung Galaxy s10, which has a pretty nice camera. I also have a little setup in my house that helps me get the lighting and shadows just right. I use natural light in all my photos. To edit, I use the VSCO app. I use one of their presets, but then I adjust things a little bit more to keep my feed cohesive.

Do you take your photos in batches, or do you take them and post them immediately?

I always take my photos in batches. Whenever I have a book launch, I usually have to wait until my book arrives before I can take photos with it. That's always a long wait! Once I get the book, I usually take a bunch of photos with it. Then I use those photos over the next few weeks/months. Sometimes I take a specific photo or two and use them right away. But I usually just do batches.

Chapter 16 : GAINING FOLLOWERS

All the advice in this book is meant to help you gain followers, and not just any followers, but the sort of community you want to build around your books. I prefer to keep my growth organic, and I do currently gain about five new followers a day with these methods. However, there are ways people use to try and gain followers more quickly.

Giveaways

Giveaways, often coupled with book tours (read more about tours in Chapter 23), can be a great way to gain followers if you make following you one of the requirements for entry. If you make sharing the post or tagging a friend another requirement, your giveaway will spread and more people will follow you to enter. It's best to give away your book, or other items targeted to the audience you want. Remember, you don't just want any followers, you want people who will be interested in your books. If your giveaway is less targeted (like an Amazon gift card), you may get more followers hoping to win it, but they will be less engaged, and many will just unfollow you after the giveaway ends.

Follow trains

The way this works is that a host (or group of hosts) will post a graphic that says "Follow Train." They then give instructions that include following the hosts, liking and saving the post, and commenting "done" in the comments. The other participants will come along and look at the comments, and if they choose to follow someone, they'll reply to their comment with "followed" and the commenter is expected to follow them back. In my opinion, this is more beneficial to host than to participate in, as you'll get more followers and won't be required to follow accounts you may not want to.

Shout-outs for Shout-outs

Often, a group of Instagrammers will get together and trade shout-outs for shout-outs. Shout-outs are posting a screenshot of the person's feed in your Stories with a link to their account. The hosts will each post a graphic in their feed, usually one advertising their combined followers. So it might say S4S or SFS (shout-outs for shout-outs), and it will give instructions. Generally, participants must follow each of the hosts, and then post a screenshot of each host's feed in their Stories for 24 hours. When they've done this, they will post "done" and tag two or three friends in a comment on the shoutout graphic post.

The hosts then go through and return shout-outs to each person by posting a screenshot of their feed. The idea is that those people get their accounts shown off by the hosts, and hopefully gain new followers through it.

This can be effective for gaining followers for both hosts and participants, but if you do nothing but share shoutouts in your Stories, some people will start skipping them.

Mass Following

This method involves following people with the hopes that they will follow you back. I don't like this method, because it's not something that's done in the bookstagram community, so those people won't generally follow you back. Other authors are more likely to follow you back (I'm pretty sure this is mostly people who use Twitter, as this works there), but are they your target audience? The other issue is that it requires you to follow so many people, that your feed becomes overwhelming and untargeted. I want to follow people who are in my community and inspire me. Lastly, mass following and then mass unfollowing can look like spam to the algorithm and you may end up locked out or unable to post for a period of time.

PART 2 - CONNECTING WITH READERS

PART 3: *Beyond the Basics*

Chapter 17 : STORIES

Stories are temporary posts that only stay up for 24 hours. They can be images or 15 second videos, and are generally more casual than your main Instagram feed. Unlike regular posts, Stories are vertical and fill up the whole phone screen. You post a story by tapping the little camera icon above your profile photo on the main feed page. Stories show up on your follower's screen as a row of profile photos with colored rings around them. The accounts they interact with the most are in that first row (not the most recent post).

If someone comments on your Stories, it goes straight to you as a direct message. But if you haven't approved the sender, they'll be shunted to your "general" or "request" tabs. Also, you can turn comments off, if you just don't want to deal with them that day.

You might see some Stories with links, but only accounts with more than 10k followers can post links in their Stories. Totally unfair? Yes it is, but those are the rules.

Instagram Stories might not seem worth the effort on the surface. You get far less eyes on your Stories than on your feed. As I write this, I have 2.8k followers. My feed posts average about 600 views, half of whom weren't following me. So...10-30% of my followers actually see each post. This is partly thanks to the mystical algorithm, but there's a lot of competition for your followers' attention as they scroll.

Fewer people watch Stories—I get maybe 60 views over the lifetime of a story.

Those 60 views are gold though. Those viewers are invested enough in you that they want to see more. They want to get to know you better. Comments on Stories are more likely to turn into conversations. And those conversations are how relationships are built.

How often should you post a story?

Ideally, you want to always have a story up. So, the minimum is every 24 hours. But you can post a lot more. The sweet spot of how many to post in a day will be up to you, but if there are too many Stories in one day, people could be overwhelmed by how many there are and just skip. There's no hard and fast rule for it. Play around and see what works for you and your audience.

Stories are casual. Don't overthink them or spend a lot of time setting them up. I'll give you some ideas in the next chapter.

Story Highlights

There is a way to keep your Stories from disappearing: put them in your highlights. Highlights are like folders that you can keep Stories in permanently. You can add to your highlights from current or archived Stories. Highlights show up on your profile page just above your photos. You can currently have an unlimited amount of highlights, with 100 Stories in each highlight.

So why use them? Highlights can be a great way for newcomers to your account to learn more about you and your books. You could have a highlight with Stories about your books, or with frequently asked reader questions, or about your cat (people love cats!).

Some tips:

- Make highlight covers. I'm not going to explain this here. You'll be better off looking it up online and reading a post with graphics showing you how. But covers make your highlights look more professional and your profile more polished. Choose covers that match your brand.

- Don't actually have millions of highlights with a hundred Stories in each. People visiting your page can only see four and a half highlight covers before they have to swipe. I wouldn't do more than ten. Really try and keep it to timeless, interesting, and/or helpful content.

- Make sure each highlight has a goal, and be purposeful about adding to it. Remember that a new follower might watch the whole thing, so you want it to make sense.

INTERVIEW WITH: *Tyffany Hackett*

Handle: @tyffany.h
Followers: 4.6k
Account style: Bookstagram (author)
Genre: YA/NA Fantasy

How long have you been on Instagram, and where were you in your publishing journey when you started?
I've been on Instagram since late 2016 and joined bookstagram shortly after. Back then I was just starting to get into the first draft of a werewolf story, one that I actually ended up putting aside a few months later to start drafting *Imber*.

Do you feel that Instagram helps you sell books? How else is it helpful to you as an author?

I don't really put as much time into any other platform, so I think Instagram—and bookstagram, more specifically—is an incredible tool to help sell books. (That I even have sales is evidence of that!) As an author, I'm grateful for the connections it's helped me form not only with readers but also with other authors.

Do you do anything special for a book launch on Instagram?

I have a street team, and usually leading up to a book launch I'll run fun challenges for them. Sometimes it's as simple as "make a post sharing my books" or "share a story or aesthetic of one of my characters." It's fun for all of us and helps them spread the word about my books with genuine enthusiasm. Fortunately, they also tend to go above and beyond, so I can't praise enough the value of having a good team of supporters around.

On top of that, I tend to share songs or aesthetics that pertain to my books, or quotes, etc. I share anything I'm tagged in with my books. Just anything and everything to continuously keep my books in the forefront of potential reader's brains. Oh, and I've started to really love the idea of release day live streams!

Which posts get the most engagement for you?
Honestly? Art prints. Always art. Which is great because art is one of my favorite things about bookstagram too. Win-win!

What's your favorite thing about the community?
I don't know any place on the internet that's as welcoming as bookstagram. Truly, people are generally just so much nicer, and we all just want to chill and talk about books. I've met some of the most wonderful, amazing friends. It's beautiful.

What do you take your photos with? Do you use any editing software?
I have an iPhone XR. I take all of my photos with that. Then I use a bunch of editing apps to tweak them! Some of my favorites are ColorStory, Snapseed, Inshot, and Mextures.

What are a couple of caption types or questions that you like best?

I'm a fan of predictive text games, to be honest. They're engaging and they usually crack me up because they're so ridiculous. But "this or that" games can be great too. They're quick, you can learn about your followers, and they really make people think!

How do you use Stories?

I use Stories primarily for more personal content. It gives me a chance to express who I am, and more of my interests, without affecting my primary feed. They're a great way of adding *you* to your account without tripping the algorithm. Stories are also where I post the majority of my writing updates and content, and they're handy for polling people if I need quick opinions on stuff.

I also feel like I should mention that I always have *something* in my Stories. I don't know if Instagram rewards that or not, but my story engagement has been steadier since I adopted that "rule."

How personal do you get on your account?

On my main feed, I don't get super personal too often. Once in a while I'll talk about my struggles with mental health or other such life things, but mostly I try to keep it book related. I do tend to post more personal stuff in my

Stories, but my Stories are also where I'm most self expressive. Because again,what you post in your Stories doesn't really affect the algorithm.

How much time do you devote to Instagram in a day or week?
Hahahahaha! Too much, honestly, and somehow still not enough. I average about four hours a day (on and off, not all at once), but sometimes it's definitely more and sometimes it's definitely less.

Do you have any advice for authors on using Instagram?
Use bookstagram. As much as I love writerly updates, writers aren't your target audience. If you're using writing related hashtags, your content is being shown to fellow writers . . . which is great for making connections but not so great if you actually want to sell your books. Separate accounts are fine! (if you wanted to do, say, writerly/personal content and then bookish content on their own pages, for instance.) But Booksta is the most effective way I personally have found to utilize Instagram as an author.
You don't need to shove your books down people's throats; post them regularly, absolutely, but post them

the same way you do other books. People really do get tired of seeing the same books over and over on a feed, and nobody likes feeling like they're being aggressively marketed to.

Be consistent. I let my account drop off for about a year and a half while I was dealing with some life stuff, and it really hurt my account. I'm only just starting to see consistent growth again. Instagram rewards consistency. That doesn't mean you have to post every day, but it does mean if you decide to post every other day or three times a day, keep a steady posting schedule. If you can post the same time every day, bonus points.

Engage in the reading community. Really engage. Don't go in expecting that every post you make is going to sell a book. Post things you enjoy. Share the love and passion for stories and characters that makes you a writer to begin with. Express yourself. Let your readers, or potential readers, get to know you. Just have fun. The rest will happen if you work hard enough. I promise.

Chapter 18: IDEAS FOR STORIES

Okay then, what should you post in your Stories?

The simplest is to just post photos you take on your phone. I often take a photo of my work area at my local cafe, or the book I'm reading. Nothing fancy, just checking in.

You can also use some of the features in Stories to ask questions, or do a poll. These are fun and quick ways for your followers to engage with you.

But those are easy—let's talk about video. Videos are a powerful way to connect with your audience. If they see your face and listen to your voice, they start to feel like they know you. And Instagram Stories are a super easy way to start getting comfortable with video. You can get used to seeing yourself on the screen and hearing the weird way your voice sounds. You can do it. Because it's in tiny fifteen-second chunks and they disappear in 24 hours.

Not everyone watches Stories with the sound on, and some of your followers may be hearing impaired, so it's a great idea to include captions. There are apps you can use to add captions, like Clipomatic, or you can just add text to your videos in the Stories creator before posting.

People expect Stories to be more casual. You don't want to waste their time, but you don't have to have a polished delivery or do your hair all perfect. I mean you can, but remember, they want to get to know you better. Don't be afraid to be authentic.

Personally, I love this tension between my very aesthetically pleasing, planned feed and my spontaneous, messy Stories. I want my feed to look gorgeous, but I wouldn't want people to believe that my life is this beautiful fairytale. That's not how you build relationships.

Daily videos are good, but even aiming for once a week is a great start.

Some ideas for your video Stories:

- updates on your writing. How far along certain projects are. How many words you got in today. What you're excited about in the story.

- unboxings of books and bookish goodies. This can be as simple as showing a book you just got off amazon. Tag the shops and authors in your video to share the love.

- share your bookshelves and some of your favorite books.

- tour of your workspace.

- a tour of your local bookstore and funny books you see there.

- I don't share a lot about my kids (I have a personal Instagram for that), but I do often show a quick video of me working at the table with my youngest daughter. It's cute and still related to my work.

- a funny story about your day (especially if you write with humor).

- one time I baked a recipe that was mentioned in my book and did Stories the whole evening, showing the process. Then I shared the cute printable recipe card that I had made for my newsletter.

- And sometimes, I just talk about my hair or outfit. It's all about what you want to share and what your audience responds to.

Another great way to use Stories is sharing posts. When you're scrolling on Instagram, you can share a post to your Stories (anyone's, including yours, as long as it's a public account) by tapping the little paper airplane icon under the photo. This opens up your Stories creator and you can add text and images to the post and then share it. Many people also share all of their own posts, to ensure that their followers don't miss them.

My favorite posts to share are art and photos that have the same feel as my books. Because I write fairytale retellings, I share a lot of castles and girls in giant dresses. I follow a few photographers that I love and share a couple of photos a day. Sometimes I'll come across a photo or illustration that looks just like one of my characters or locations, and I'll be sure to mention that when I share it.

I love that I can easily share beautiful images and that it always links back to the original post. As an illustrator, I know how hard it is when your work gets shared around without recognition (saying you found it on Pinterest doesn't mean anything, my friends). So this is a way to share something you love while helping the creator grow their audience as well.

I also support my author buddies by sharing their posts about their book launches, cover reveals, and sales in my Stories.

And always, always share any posts that include your book, and mention the account that shared it so they can see the story in their messages. This does two things: It makes you look cool (look, people love my book!) and it shows gratitude to your reader and builds a better relationship with them. It doesn't matter if the photo is gorgeous or not, share it.

There are more things that happen in Stories. Memes, giveaways, and shop announcements, to name a few. Just start watching and you'll have more ideas than you know what to do with.

INTERVIEW WITH: *Faroukh Naseem*

Handle: @theguywiththebook
Followers: 60.4k
Account style: Bookstagram (influencer)

When did you start your account?
Back in August 2015!

Which posts get the most engagement for you?
It's a little confusing how Instagram works, but usually bookshelves posts work best. Most readers just love looking at books and books and books!

What's your favorite thing about the community?

I think Bookstagram is a very accepting place and we have all sorts of accounts. I know highly successful accounts which focus just on pictures of books and no real commitment to captions and discussion but also accounts which have engaging captions but don't focus much on aesthetics. My personal favorite accounts are those which balance both pictures and captions!

Do you have a strategy for balancing the sort of posts you make?

My page is a bit random, especially during the lockdown earlier this year in Saudi Arabia. There was a 3 month period where I couldn't go out and take my usual books in café pictures, so I had to change my content to focus more on pictures at home. But usually I try to have a mix of café, home, bookstores and book shelf pictures!

What do you take your photos with? Do you use any editing software?

I use my phone which has a great camera. There was a period where I took a lot of pictures using a mirrorless camera as well, but I'm more comfortable just pointing and shooting with the phone (It's a bit easier taking phone pictures in public too, cameras bring too much attention!!). For editing, I just use the built-in filters of Instagram (I use "Ludwig" the most) and play around with different settings.

Do you take your photos in batches, or do you take them and post them immediately?

Yes, on weekends I visit a café and take around 10-15 postable pictures. I carry around a dozen books, some of which I have read and some that I'm planning to read in the coming weeks. I might not post all of them in, say, the coming month—sometimes I post a picture 2-3 months later too, especially if it's a book I intended to read but didn't really get to (which happens...a lot!).

What are a couple of caption types or questions that you like best?

Captions, for me, play a great part in enjoying Bookstagram. If I have a picture with 5000 likes, but only 10-20 comments, it's just not as satisfying as a picture which might have 1000 likes but 40-50 comments. I make sure to include an emoji where my question is in the caption so it's easier for people to notice and respond. My favorite question is when people ask about Bookmarks vs Dogearing books – it's bound to create some fun drama!

Do you read all the books you post on your feed?

No, I include a lot of books that I'm excited to read as well. I wouldn't get to post much if I only posted about books I read! When I'm in the mood to discuss something in general about reading, I'll post a picture of an open book or a bookshelf!

How personal do you get on your account?

I try not to get too personal. I've realized that communicating on social media through text or even videos loses a lot of nuance and people might not really get what I'm trying to say (if it's a serious topic). But also, I'm not really someone who likes discussing his private life much. I might be having a bad day, but my posts just might not show it! I like Bookstagram to be just a place to escape sometimes.

Do you have any tips for creating a cohesive theme?

What's worked for me is that I have a few types of pictures that I take: café table, book shelves, on the bed, wrist in frame. I just keep mixing them up, and over time, I've gotten a bit better at knowing how they would come together! Best tip is to keep posting and keep experimenting! You never know what'll work! Overall, keep it fun, do it for you!

Chapter 19: LIVE

L ive videos are a lot like Stories, but are—wait for it—live! When you start a Live video, your followers will be notified and they can pop in and watch. Even if they don't choose to watch your Live, this can be a reminder that your account is out there. Anyone watching your videos can leave comments in the chat and give hearts. While you're streaming live, your avatar will be at the top of your follower's feeds, just like with Stories, but it will be in front of all the Stories with a "Live" tag.

Live videos can be up to an hour long and you can post them to your IGTV channel when you're done so that anyone who missed it can check it out later. Currently however, you can't edit them, so try not to have a long dead space at the beginning while you wait for people to join, if you're planning to keep the video. It's better to introduce yourself and your topic right away, even if people are still joining. You can always repeat your intro later.

Something I love about Live videos is that you can invite someone to join you and the screen splits between you for your viewers. This means that you can do interviews or discuss a topic with another author or reader.

Live is also great for question-and-answer videos, because you can take questions from the chat. It can be a good idea to ask for questions in your Stories in advance so you have a few planned to get things rolling, but it's so fun to answer questions live. This can be really fun for a book launch.

Instagram seems to be making it harder and harder to do long videos in Stories, so I've found myself using Live more often lately. Even if there is only one or two people watching, it's an easy way to make a casual, slightly longer video which you can then save as an IGTV.

I'm still figuring out the best way to use Live streams, but I know some authors do them once a week and get great engagement. Play with it and see what works for you!

INTERVIEW WITH: *Briana Morgan*

Handle: @brianamorganbooks
Followers: 9.5k
Account style: Bookstagram/Author
Genre: Horror

How long have you been on Instagram, and where were you in your publishing journey when you started?
I've been on Instagram since 2010, but when I started my account, it was just a personal Instagram. I didn't start using it as my author Instagram until shortly before I released my debut novel in 2015.

Do you feel that Instagram helps you sell books? How else is it helpful to you as an author?

SO many of my sales come from Instagram, and it's also helped me discover more horror readers and reviewers! I can't say enough good things about using Instagram as an author. I've even managed to generate business for my editing and publishing consulting services there as well.

Do you do anything special for a book launch on Instagram?

In the past, I've done themed prompts for each day leading up to the book's release with a paperback giveaway at the end. I also host an Instagram live launch party, where I answer questions and talk about the book.

Which posts get the most engagement for you?

Posts where I'm showing off my book covers or talking about other people's books!

What's your favorite thing about the community?

I love how supportive everyone is and how willing people are to promote indie authors, especially in the horror niche.

Do you have a strategy for balancing the sort of posts you make?

I look at my feed as I'm coming up with posts and try to refrain from posting two similar pictures in a row. Also, I try not to promote my work so much that it's annoying. It's all about balance.

What do you take your photos with? Do you use any editing software?

I just take photos with my phone, the Pixel 4A. I use VSCO to edit my photos.

How personal do you get on your account?

I'm all about transparency, and my honesty has helped me build and deepen my relationships with other people on the platform. However, I try to avoid sharing things that might be gross or emotionally manipulative in some way, as those are the kinds of posts that turn me off in other people's feeds. Really, though, you should only be as personal as you're comfortable with.

How much time do you devote to Instagram in a day or week?

Too much. I'm on there at least an hour every day.

Do you have any advice for authors on using Instagram?

Seek out and engage with readers, rather than just other writers. Readers are more likely to be interested in your work.

Chapter 20: IGTV

I have a confession for you. I barely use IGTV. As I said in the beginning, you can't and shouldn't do everything. Not if you want to have time to keep writing books. And this is something I've chosen not to do. But here are some facts to get you started:

IGTV is basically Instagram's answer to YouTube (because Instagram is owned by Facebook, and they pretty much want to take over the world. Just ask Snapchat). It's currently for videos up to ten minutes long, or an hour for the bigger accounts. These videos can be viewed in the main Instagram app, or in the standalone IGTV app.

It used to be only vertical video (like Stories), but they've updated it to allow for horizontal video as well. Which means that if you are already making videos for YouTube, you can repurpose them for IGTV.

Like with Stories, you can be less polished than a YouTube video, but you don't have to. Both ways work. I've seen a lot of accounts start to use IGTV the same way they use Stories, but without having to break everything into one minute chunks.

You can repost your Live videos as IGTV videos (this is all I've used it for so far).

In my experience, people don't watch IGTV as regularly as Stories, so if you post one, I would put a snippet in your Stories. IGTV videos are stored in their own section on your profile. You can also add it to your main feed so it shows up for your followers when they're scrolling. I like to remove mine after a day because they don't look as pretty, but you can get around this by uploading a custom cover to match your feed.

You can organize your videos into episodes in a series, and hashtags and comments work the same as with regular Instagram.

Some ideas for IGTV:

- Do a reading from your books

- Cook a recipe linked to your books

- Show off your pretty hardback editions

- Explore a location that inspired your story

- All the video ideas I gave you for Stories, but longer

INTERVIEW WITH: *Valia Lind*

Handle: @valialind
Followers: 1.7k
Account style: Bookstagram (author)
Genre: YA Urban Fantasy

How long have you been on Instagram, and where were you in your publishing journey when you started?

I've been on Instagram for eight years now. My first post was in 2012, with a picture of a coffee mug. I wasn't publishing back then, and it would be another two years before my first self-pub book came out. I was a writer though. My first post caption was "#amwriting with my trusty coffee by my side."

What do you take your photos with? Do you use any editing software?

I take the majority of my photos with my iPhone X. In the past I've used my DSLR, but that's very rarely now. For edits, I use Lightroom and Instasize for the border.

Do you take your photos in batches, or do you take them and post them immediately?

That really depends on my week. I try to have at least a few photos stocked up, but I often end up taking photos on the spot and sharing that. This is different when I have a book coming out, or cover reveals scheduled. I like to stay as close to the "insta" part as I can.

What's your favorite thing about the community?

I really do love how open and artistic it is. I mean, readers and writers are both approachable (for the most part), and their personalities can be seen through their pictures. We're all taking pictures of books, but each has their own touch, and I love that. It really helps to get to know the community better. I haven't had any drama or bad experiences within the community (which is refreshing).

Do you have a strategy for balancing the sort of posts you make?

I wouldn't say a specific strategy. I just try to keep true to the kind of posts I like to see on my feed, and go from there.

How personal do you get on your account?

I'd say I'm pretty personal, without being too much. In the past, I've shared my struggles, professionally and personally, but I don't use the platform as a dumping ground. I want my followers to feel like we're friends, but I also understand that I'm not coming in for a therapy session every time I post. If that makes sense.

How much time do you devote to Instagram in a day or week?

I typically spend about ten minutes a day posting and figuring out the caption. But I also have a day where I plan out those extra shots, so I'd say about an hour to two hours a week.

You're one of the early adopters of Reels. Why did you decide to jump in on doing them?

I actually really love videos. I had a YouTube channel at one time. I'm not comfortable in front of a camera at all, and this was a way to push myself outside of my comfort zone. It also lets me be a little bit more silly than I would be if it was a ten minute video. The short format really works for me.

How have Reels helped your account grow, and are they attracting the sort of followers you want?

As of right now, I haven't seen any huge growth from just my Reels. But I do feel like they reach a very good number of people, so I hope as I build on it, I'll start seeing more results. I feel like that's how it is with any new tech or avenue. It takes a bit of time.

How do you come up with ideas for your Reels?

I have no idea. Some came from watching others use a specific sound. Some have been from me having a conversation with my mom and acting stupid—and then saying I should do a writer version of that and her agreeing. I have a few songs that I want to use soon with some clear ideas. After that, we shall see.

Chapter 21: REELS

Instagram is always changing. I was almost done writing this book when all of a sudden, they rolled out Reels. So, let me tell you, I'm not an expert yet. But I did manage to interview two authors who are doing a great job with them.

What are they? Instagram Reels were inspired by TikTok, so a lot of people will say "Just use Reels like TikTok!"

Do you use TikTok? Nope? Me neither.

So, let me translate that for you. Reels are short, fun videos that you hope will go viral. There is a bigger emphasis on being a bit clever with them.

It's basically a little video editing app within Instagram that lets you splice together videos and images into a short video. You can use filters and effects, and you can add music from their library of popular songs.

Reels can be posted to your feed or Stories so that your viewers will see them, then they show up on your profile in your Reels section.

Reels are a great way to show your fun side and create little promos for your books in an entertaining way.

Ways I've seen Reels used include:

- your TBR (to be read) goals for the month

- a wrap-up of books you read that month

- answer frequently asked questions

- fun facts about your books

- relatable author moments

- behind the scenes of a photoshoot

- a quick overview of the books you've written

- a character cosplay

INTERVIEW WITH: *J.M. Buckler*

Handle: @author_j.m.buckler
Followers: 12k
Account style: Bookstagram (author)
Genre: YA Fantasy

How long have you been on Instagram, and where were you in your publishing journey when you started?
I started my author handle in 2017 but didn't take Instagram seriously until mid 2018.

What's a mistake you see authors making on Instagram?

Endless self-promotion. Authors need to understand that these types of posts bore their followers. Stop posting cheesy mockups of your book. Stop posting about what you ate for breakfast. Stop posting random pictures of your dog. No one cares. You do not have celebrity status. Leave random moments about your personal life off your grid. If you want to share clips of your vacation, then upload them to your Stories.

No one likes door-to-door salesmen. Stop sending authors/bookstagrammers DMs telling rather than asking them to read your book. It's rude. This tactic rarely works. Honestly, it makes me NOT want to read your book.

Think like a reader, not an author. Ask yourself why you joined Instagram. If you joined to connect with readers, then think like a reader. Aesthetic is EVERYTHING on Instagram. Take the time to learn photo editing. There are plenty of apps in the marketplace that can help your images stand out. Post pictures of books beside your own. Ask questions in your post. Engage with your audience. It's called social media for a reason. Start socializing.

Which posts get the most engagement for you?

People love faces. In my experience, I have learned that when I post a unique selfie, I get more engagement. This is a standard rule for Instagram. Now, this doesn't mean I only post selfies. I follow a pattern with my posts. Four bookish posts for one selfie. Post with a purpose.

Do you have a strategy for balancing the sort of posts you make?

Yes. I use the Planner app to organize my grid. This is a helpful tool because it allows you to preview your post before posting. I follow a theme based on the season. You must keep things fresh on Instagram. Followers get bored easily. You must keep them guessing what comes next while staying cohesive.

How personal do you get on your account?

I share my writing journey and small parts of my personal life in my Stories, but not on my grid. My author handle is strictly business. I'm not a verified account. No one cares what I ate for breakfast.

How much time do you devote to Instagram in a day or week?

On average, I spend around 3.5 hours a day on Instagram. I spread out this time, making sure I answer DMs and comments organically.

You're one of the early adopters of Reels. Why did you decide to jump in on doing them?

Reels is a feature that Instagram introduced in the late summer of 2020. Instagram rewards those who use their additional features, so I jumped on the opportunity. It's an excellent way to gain exposure.

How have Reels helped your account grow, and are they attracting the sort of followers you want?

Yes! Once I started using Reels, my follower count and engagements spiked. I gained 3,000 followers in 3 weeks. Before Reels, I was gaining around 25 new followers a month. I alternate my Reels, so they cater to both readers and authors. This allows me to attract the followers I want.

How do you come up with ideas for your Reels?

The ideas for my Reels are very spontaneous. For my author Reels, I take moments from my writing journey. I enjoy making people laugh. Followers tell me they find these Reels relatable, and they make them smile. For my reader Reels, I document moments that every reader experiences. You must think outside of the box. Lots of people make the mistake of copying other people's Reels. Don't do this. Be creative. Be inventive.

Do you have any advice for authors on using Instagram?

Execution is everything. Don't be lazy. Don't fall into the trap of copying others or posting without a purpose. Time is money. Make every post count. Don't push your books into people's faces. Promote yourself without "promoting" yourself. Take the time to learn about photography. Lighting is everything. Think like a reader. Remind yourself why you joined social media. You started playing the Instagram game as soon as you created your handle. Don't be afraid to take risks. Use Instagram's features. Post at least six days a week, use Stories daily, create IGTV videos, create Reels. You must be consistent to grow your account. Deep breaths, you've got this.

PART 4: *Influencers & Book Tours*

INSTAGRAM FOR FICTION AUTHORS

Chapter 22: INFLUENCERS

An influencer is someone who has a large following, and whose followers trust them for recommendations. Most influencers in the book community are bookstagrammers, but there are also authors and artists whose opinions pull a lot of weight with their audiences.

I generally think that while becoming an influencer might seem like something to strive for, it shouldn't be your goal as an author. Growing a large following takes a lot of effort, and most writers don't have the time to put that sort of energy into it while still successfully publishing books.

Most of the top bookstagrammers post 2-3 times every day. They review a lot of books, often sent to them by publishers, and they rep for a number of companies (more on repping in Chapter 24). They spend hours a day on it, between taking the photos, posting, and interacting with the community.

We want to build our platform, but don't aim to become a top influencer. Aim to build relationships with them, and ask for their help in getting your books in front of a bigger audience than you could ever reach on your own.

How should you contact an influencer?

First, have a look at their account. You want to collaborate with someone who has a good following and regularly posts books in your genre. Follower count is a good way to gauge how much reach they have, but remember, engagement and targeting are just as important.

Taking the time to follow them, and comment on their posts and Stories before you contact them, is a great idea. People are more likely to listen to requests from someone they recognize. Also, if you comment on their Stories, you'll show up in their DMs. This will remind them that you've spoken before and increases the odds that you won't get lost in their "general" DM folder. You can also check their profile for an email address to contact them.

Then, when you contact them, obviously be polite. Be friendly, and remember that they have a lot of obligations every month. I'm not even that big of an account, and it drives me crazy when people give me the "opportunity" to help them with a cover reveal or launch tour. Even if you are offering them a free book (even a paperback, even with cool swag), you are the one asking for a favor, not granting one. They are often drowning in free books from publishers and book boxes.

If you want help with a cover reveal, I'd show them the cover in private when you ask, even if you haven't posted it anywhere yet. Indie covers especially can be a mixed bag, and they will be more likely to agree to post yours if it's professional and matches their aesthetic.

Should you offer to send a paperback?

You can. Paperbacks photograph better than e-books. However, the influencer might be just as happy to have the cover image. Many bookstagrammers are tech savvy enough to put together a mockup of your book that looks like the real thing. This is especially helpful for cover reveals when you may not have books available yet.

I've seen some authors put together a mockup with a transparent background for bookstagrammers to insert in a photo that they take, and this can work well. It's best to use an image that would work in flat lay because those are the easiest to fake.

Most bookstagrammers who help you out won't read the book unless they're really interested. They share more books than they read. So, offer a copy (print or ebook—it's up to you and your budget) but don't ask for a review. And don't be offended if they choose not to read it. They might think their audience will be interested in your book, even if they don't have time to check it out themselves, and that's what you're really asking for.

What if someone reaches out to you?

As you get more established, both as an author and an Instagrammer, you'll start to have people reach out and ask for books. They'll offer to post your books on their feed, to give you more visibility. So, should you do it?

While it can be helpful to have more posts about your books out in the world of Instagram, some people are not going to be a good fit. Some people just want free books. And some even ask you to pay them to review your books. You can decide on a case-by-case basis if you're going to send them a book, but it might be helpful to have a criteria worked out in advance.

Here's mine:

- I don't send books to people who ask me to pay for their services. Ever. I highly doubt that they have enough reach to sell enough of my books with one post to make that money back. I can do a better job of that myself, and after reading this book, so can you! One bookstagrammer, no matter how many followers, is not that valuable. It's more about having people see your books on many feeds over time. So if someone asks, I simply say that it's not something I'm currently doing.

- I don't send a free paperback to anyone who doesn't seem like an exceptional fit for my book. The bookstagrammers big enough to really get my books noticed are busy enough that they are not going to reach out to me. I'll have to reach out to them. Occasionally, a paperback might be worth shipping to a mid-range influencer (at least 10k followers and good engagement) if they regularly post books similar enough to mine that their followers might be into my book.

- I do, however, offer an ebook to anyone who offers to feature my book on their feed. Most people only want the paperback and decline my offer. That's fine by me, because I know how to create buzz on Instagram without paying a lot of money to anyone or sending paperbacks out to everyone who asks.

INTERVIEW WITH: *Audrey Grey*

Handle: @audreygreyauthor
Followers: 5.8k
Account style: Author
Genre: YA Fantasy

How long have you been on Instagram, and where were you in your publishing journey when you started?

I've been on Instagram since February 2016. I was newly published and joined because my publisher suggested it, but I didn't actually take my Instagram platform seriously until I published independently in 2019.

Do you feel that Instagram helps you sell books? How else is it helpful to you as an author?

Instagram is an amazing platform for reaching dedicated readers in your genre—particularly Young Adult readers—and growing your brand awareness.

As far as selling books, if an author builds their presence on Instagram expecting immediate, tangible sales, they may be disappointed. While there certainly is an uptick in print book sales once your platform is big enough, for the most part, I've found that Instagram is much more effective for growing brand awareness and name recognition than selling books. It's one necessary facet in a much larger marketing strategy. The results are hard to quantify, but important for long term success as an author.

What's your experience with using book tours as part of your Instagram strategy? Have they helped you gain new readers?

I was lucky to have a personal assistant for the last year who ran my book tours and connected with bookstagrammers on my behalf. She was directly responsible for growing my Instagram profile and connections, which in turn resulted in more exposure and readers. I think book tours are great, especially if you go into them with the right expectations. Will they immediately sell a ton of books for you? Probably not. But they do have the potential to reach new readers and strengthen your brand recognition.

Which posts get the most engagement for you?
In my experience, posts that feature myself in some form get the most engagement. I think people are naturally curious about the person behind the pictures and respond more readily to those types of personalized images.

What's your favorite thing about the community?
My favorite thing about the Instagram book community is the passion for literature as well as acceptance. I think readers are more open and empathetic to those who don't conform to society's expectations, and therefore much more supportive to creative types.

What do you take your photos with? Do you use any editing software?
For now, I use my iPhone and sometimes templates from Bookbrush. Otherwise, my setups are pretty low-key.

Do you take your photos in batches, or do you take them and post them immediately?

I post less than I'd like—once every week or two—so currently I take my photos and post immediately. But if and when I can post more frequently, I'll probably take the images in batches.

How personal do you get on your account?

I definitely personalize my posts as much as possible when informing my followers about upcoming releases or sales, but I keep it very professional. Just like all forms of social media, it can be very easy to use Instagram as a social outlet, but I do think you have to separate the personal from the professional.

How much time do you devote to Instagram in a day or week?

Currently, I don't devote very much time to my profile. Maybe thirty minutes a week. I do think the more time you put in to building up your network and connections, the more you'll get out of Instagram.

Do you have any advice for authors on using Instagram?

My advice to other authors would be to find a theme or aesthetic that aligns with your brand and make sure your posts consistently reflect that aesthetic. Consistent branding is the key to ensuring your message stays clear and reaches the most people.

Chapter 23: BOOK TOURS

Book tours are a very effective way to spread the word about your book around the bookstagram community. This is where a bunch of accounts post about your book, either on a given day (usually for a cover reveal) or over the course of a week, to build buzz. Week-long tours can be more effective than one-day events, because it looks more organic and gives the impression that your book is everywhere.

You may have heard the advertising adage that people need to see something seven times before they'll buy it. It may take more than seven times for someone to even remember your book exists, but the more their respected peers and influencers post about a book, the more enticing it becomes.

You can hire a company to run a tour for you (check out the next interview for one!). I do think that an Instagram tour is a great use of your advertising money, but you can also do it yourself if you want to. I prefer to keep my money and make the connections myself. Other authors prefer to leave it to someone else and save that time for writing. Both options are good choices, but whichever you choose, think about running a tour for your next book launch.

How I set up a tour

It's going to be tricky to run your own tour if you don't have an established presence on Instagram, because it's all about the people who want to see you succeed and are willing to help you out. It also helps to have a really appealing book.

You'll need to organize a group of accounts to help you. This can include: author friends, your followers, readers of your previous books, your street team if you have one, and influencers you might seek out individually.

Collect their email addresses and send them your book cover and any important information about it (blurb, release date, pre-order offers, any specific hashtags you want used). Then tell them which day you'd like them to post (if you're working with big accounts, you may need to ask them about their schedule).

Pretty simple!

My current Instagram launch strategy

I'm putting together an anthology launch as I'm writing this, and I thought I'd lay out for you in more detail what I'm trying out. It's more in depth than just a single book tour.

1) Set-up.

I set up a Google form to send interested people to. This is less work for me but more work for them, so I might get less replies than by just telling people to comment if they're interested. However, this book is an anthology and all eight authors will be asking for help, so we needed a central place to send people. The form collects a name, Instagram handle, email address, and asks which of three things they want to help with: Cover reveal, ARCs, and launch week tour. All the authors involved put the link to this form as our website link in our bio.

2) Title reveal and call for help.

I made a square graphic that showed the title off. It had a blurred-out background that matches the cover and the sparkly title text. All eight of us posted the image in our feeds, either as a first image or as a second slider with a main image that matched our theme better (but still related to the book). We called this post a "Title Reveal" and announced the book while sending people to the link if they were interested in helping out. We also shared this in our Stories. Doing this at least twice is best, as people often miss a post, even if they follow you.

3) Reach out to individuals you want to work with.

If there are friends or influencers you want to help you out, DM them directly and ask. Go back and read the chapter about contacting influencers if you need to. If there are authors you've helped in the past (which you should!), this is a good time to ask them if they can reciprocate. Send them to your form as well.

4) Arrange the cover reveal.

Set up your cover reveal by emailing the dates, cover image, and any other info to the people who signed up to help, at least a week in advance. Even more time is better, as they may need time to take photos. You can create a mockup of your book on a transparent background to help them out. You can also make up square graphics for them to add to their slider of images with the book release date and any pre-order info. That makes it easier for them to get the information you want out to their followers.

I have previously mailed out prints of the cover image and pre-order swag to people helping with my reveal. This isn't a terrible idea, but in the future, I think I'll only mail physical objects to people who are willing to join my street team. You could also enter the participants in a giveaway to win a copy of the book or some fun swag.

5) Send out ARCs to anyone who requested them (I think you can never have too many ARC readers, but that's a personal preference).

6) Cover reveal tour.

In addition to posting the cover on your own feed, be sure to visit all the tour members posts and comment on them. Gush over their photos. Add every post to your Stories and tag the poster (otherwise they may not see it). This makes your book look popular and is a great way to thank the people who participate in your tour.

If you only have an e-book pre-order, encourage anyone who asks about paperbacks to join your newsletter for a notification when the paperback is released.

7) Set up and run the launch tour.

This will be very similar to your cover reveal tour, but hopefully some of the tour members will have read your ARC and be able to include a short review. If you're keeping your book at a lower price for launch week, be sure to have them include that in their post. Be aware that the bookstagram community likes paperbacks, so it's helpful to have your paperback ready to go at the same time as the ebook launch (or earlier if you want to collect reviews). Interact just as much as you did during the cover reveal tour.

That's it! Hopefully that will give your book a good boost for its pre-order and launch. Remember that just like anywhere, you'll get the best results with a gorgeous cover and killer blurb.

INTERVIEW WITH: *Storygram Tours*

Owners: Bridget (@darkfaerietales_)
and Kristen (@myfriendsarefiction)
Handle: @storygramtours for YA
@storygramkids for children's and MG
Website: www.storygramtours.com
Followers: 94.5k

How did Storygram Tours get started?

We started when Bridget asked Kristen to help run a fun tour for a book she loved. Bridget thought it would be cool to do something like a blog tour but on Instagram. We had so much fun working together that we decided to start the business. We had met at a bookish convention and hit it off so well that we became fast best friends.

What exactly is a book tour, and why is it so valuable?

Our Instagram tours are similar in structure to a blog tour with a group of tour hosts that each feature the tour book on a specific date. So a tour might run 7 days and one tour host posts per day. They tag the person that will post the following day which creates a loop for people to follow along with daily. Instagram is one of the most popular social networking sites and reaches a vast audience, so we feel it is a valuable place to get a book seen. The more a book is seen, the more likely a consumer will buy it if they see it in a bookstore or on an online site. With our tours, we market the books in a fun and unique way that doesn't feel like an ad.

Do your tours include blogs and YouTube, or are they strictly Instagram based?

Our tours are Instagram based as of right now. We have been utilizing IGTV more since it has gained popularity.

Do you work with indie authors, or only traditionally published books?

We do work with indie authors on a case-by-case basis depending on if we feel the book is a good fit for our audience. We generally find the most success with YA crossover books or anything fantasy (bookstagrammers really love fantasy, lol).

How do you select the books you feature in your tours?
We look at the genre of the book as well as the author's previous work, the cover (since Instagram is such a visual media), and the summary.

When do you think book tours are most valuable? Before launch, during the release week, or anytime?
We offer an ARC tour, which runs a few months prior to release date, which are very popular for getting the word out about pre-order campaigns as well as getting the community excited about the book. Release day tours are great because people are able to get the book immediately when interested. We do have a lot of luck with tours later on too. I honestly don't think there is a bad time to market.

Do you do cover reveals and e-book tours, or only print books?
We do cover reveals when our schedule allows for it (for these, we like to see the cover and summary). We have really started doing more e-book tours in recent months.

I do think physical books allow for the most creative pictures, so we tend to prefer them over e-books.

Do you have any advice for authors who do a tour to get the most out of the experience?

I think being engaged with the tour is a great way to get the most out of the experience. Obviously having a public Instagram account where you feature information about your book is great so that we can link to it. We also suggest a giveaway which allows entrants to gain entries by following your account. Many of our clients repost tour pictures in their story or on their account to also let their current followers know a tour is going on.

Chapter 24: REPRESENTING OTHER BUSINESSES

Okay, let's look at the other side of the influencer coin for a moment. As your Instagram account grows, you may start to get requests from companies to show off their products in your feed—usually in return for a free product, occasionally for money. Depending on the product, this can be pretty tempting.

Also, there are a lot of companies selling "bookish merch" or book related merchandise in the bookstagram community. Everything from book boxes (which we'll look at closer in the next chapter) to candles, bookmarks, and T-shirts. These companies often have "rep searches" where they'll ask people who are interested in representing their brand to post a sampling of their best photos along with a specific hashtag. The company goes through the hashtag to look at the entries, then picks a handful of accounts to send free products to in return for posting photos of them. Those accounts are their "reps" or representatives.

So, is repping a fun way to get some free candles, or does it make you look like a sell-out? If you're interested in repping but want to make sure it aligns with your author goals, here are some things to think about:

Does the product align with your brand?

If you write thrillers, maybe promoting picture books on your feed would be a bit confusing. On the other hand, tea is part of my brand. I love tea. It shows up in all my books, and I use teacups and teapots as props in nearly half my photos. So, working with a bookish tea company was a fun fit for my brand.

What are the requirements?

Is this a one time thing? Or are you agreeing to post twice a week and share daily in your Stories? How much of your feed will this take over, and is it worth it? This could depend on how often you post and how many brands you end up working with.

Is this a company that you'd like to build a relationship with?

Repping can be a great way to get to know a company and could (note "could") lead to future collaborations. I ended up doing a very fun illustration commission for a book box that I rep for.

There are more ways to look at it, for sure. In general, just think about how you want to present yourself and what sort of relationships you want to build. Repping can make you look cool (you got picked!) but it can also dilute your brand if you're promoting things other than your book.

As I write this, I'm repping for two companies. BooksnLeaf is a bookish tea company that I chose to work with because...I love tea and books. It's a small business based in my province and aligns well with my brand. I buy from them anyway.

Owlcratejr is a middle grade book box. I honestly do this one for my kids who love the books and the curated goodies that come with them. Middle grade is a bit lower than my target audience of clean YA, but there's a lot of overlap. And as I mentioned earlier, I did get illustration work from them.

On the other hand, I was picked in a rep search for another book box and realized that I would have to post 12 rep posts a month between the three companies. Way too many. I shouldn't have applied for it and ended up passing, which might have burned a potential client relationship.

Deciding whether to rep or not, and who to collaborate with, is not something to do on a whim. Think it through, and decide if it's worth it or not.

Free Books

Similar to repping is accepting free books. Publishers often send out advance reader copies to bookstagrammers and, as you read in the book tour section, indies sometimes do as well. This is much more likely to happen if you live in the US (because of shipping). Having an advance copy of a hot upcoming book can get you some very nice attention on bookstagram, but again, make sure you know what's required of you (do you have to read it? Do you have time to read it? Do you need to post a nice review, even if you don't like it?).

Personally, no one wants to send me books because I live in Canada. I've made my peace with it. At least I have a hot Prime Minister.

INTERVIEW WITH: *Christine Manzari*

Handle: @xenatine
Followers: 77k
Account style: Bookstagram (author/influencer)
Genre: YA Academy/NA Romance

How long have you been on Instagram, and where were you in your publishing journey when you started?

I've been on Instagram since soon after it was created, but I didn't make my account purely book related until May 2016. I self-published my first book in August 2013, so I had a few self-published books under my belt by the time I started doing bookstagram. I initially started doing bookstagram as a way to reach new readers and promote my books, but once I started doing photo challenges and engaging with other book lovers, I found I was promoting other authors more than myself. To be honest, I'll go months without featuring my own books sometimes because there are just so many good books out there to talk about.

Which posts get the most engagement for you?

Shelfie posts get a lot of engagement for me, but the ones that seem to get the most engagement are those that feature popular authors and series like Sarah J. Maas, Cassandra Clare, Leigh Bardugo, and Holly Black. Even though I know posting those books all the time would do well for me, I post about them sparingly. I like to post a variety of books and authors, so I'm concerned more about sharing books I love and am excited about than with ones that I know will get huge engagement. I still post those from time to time because I love them, but there are a lot of books and authors I want my followers to get to know, so I mix it up.

What's your favorite thing about the community?

My favorite thing about the bookstagram community is being able to gush over my favorite stories and help people discover new books to obsess over. I also love that because bookstagram is digital, it's like having pen pals all over the world. It's pretty wild to say "My friend in Germany loves that book, too." Bookstagram has given us the ability to be friends no matter where we live.

What do you take your photos with? Do you use any editing software?

I use my iPhone 10 to take photos. Sometimes I will use Afterlight, Snapseed, or Pixaloop to adjust the photo or add animation, but I don't do it often. Usually I rely on taking photos with natural light and editing them within Instagram if they need to be lighter or less saturated. I've been thinking about finding a filter to use, but I sort of like that my photos are natural and all me. I think I have commitment issues with using a filter.

Do you take your photos in batches, or do you take them and post them immediately?

I usually take pictures three days a week, and on each of those days, I'll take a bunch to last me a few days. But sometimes life gets busy and I have to take a photo right before I need to post it for a tour. I do like to plan my photos out though. I keep a calendar for tours I'm on and I have a list of books from publishers that I need to promote. Every Sunday, I make a list of what photos I need to take for the week, and with the help of some photo challenges, I'll jot down notes of what sorts of layouts I might use.

You rep for a few different companies and participate in book tours. How do you balance those responsibilities with your personal posts?

I am a lover of lists, so I keep a calendar for my tours and I keep lists for rep posts. Everything is well planned out every week when it comes to bookstagram.

When I don't have a rep post, book tour, or publisher sponsored post to do, I like to feature books I love and often use photo challenges as inspiration for which books to feature.

You've had your book featured in a book box. How did that work, and do you feel it was helpful in selling copies of your book (or was it useful in other ways)?

I was so honored to have Faecrate ask me to include my ebook in their box. I love that they really try to promote indie authors. I gave the ebook away as a free download in that box so I didn't really sell more copies because of being included, but I feel it did help to introduce more readers to my book, which is always a good thing. Especially for a series that's been out as long as mine has.

How do you choose if you're going to promote a book?
I get asked to promote a lot of books, and sadly, I have to tell some authors and publishers no because I can't possibly feature all the ones I get offered. First, the book has to be of interest to me, something I would want to read. Since I mostly read YA fantasy, scifi, paranormal, and romcom, those are easy sells for me. I do enjoy adult and new adult books that fall in those categories, but I'll often decline to feature horror, thriller, mystery, and non-fiction no matter what age group it is.

If it's something that sounds good and I'm not familiar with the author already, I'll usually check Goodreads to see what the ratings and reviews are if it has any. I find that my preferences usually fall in line well with Goodreads ratings. I usually enjoy books with ratings 3.8 and higher. Sometimes I will feature books that I might not want to read but I think might interest my followers—like middle grade and children's books. But if I choose a book to feature, it means that I'd like to read it. I really want my promotion of books to be genuine. Even if I'm not reading it right away, if I'm sharing a book on my account, it's because I want to read it.

Do you have any advice for authors on how to approach influencers?

I'm glad you asked this because there is definitely a wrong way that will immediately turn me off. If an author has never once interacted with me on bookstagram and sends me a DM with a link to their book asking me to buy it and feature it, I will immediately delete their message without even a reply. That kind of request is extremely offensive because it shows me that they don't value my time and what I do to promote a book. They want me to buy it AND promote it? What value is in it for me? Why would I spend my money and time on them when they haven't ever interacted with me?

Even if an author is really nice and offers to send me their book for free, if they haven't ever engaged with me (ie. commented on any of my photos or responded to my Stories) the answer is likely a no. And it's not that I don't want to help out and am not grateful for their offer, but as I said before, I get offered a lot of books and I'm going to be more likely to say yes if the author has taken the time to get to know me and interact with me. My best advice would be to invest the time with influencers and get to know them before you ask them to help you.

The other thing I would suggest is if you've messaged the influencer on bookstagram, follow up with a professional email. A few months ago, I got an amazing request from Beck Michaels to feature her book and I was so impressed with how professional her letter was that I couldn't say no.

She started out the letter by talking about my bookstagram (always a good idea to say why you like the influencer you're asking a favor from). Then she gave a nice one line pitch about the book, and she included a lovely bookstagram photo of her beautiful book (it made me want to have the book too). She also included the synopsis, and then listed her accomplishments (the book boxes her book had been included in, the reviews it had already gotten, and the tour company she was using at the time to promote it).

I was so impressed. She convinced me to say yes because she did all the work for me. Instead of just asking me to feature her book, she gave me all the reasons I wanted to. Often someone will just mention their book in a message and I have to go hunt it down on goodreads to find the synopsis and ratings. Don't do that. If you want someone to do you a favor, make it easy for them to say yes. Treat your request to an influencer like you would treat a query letter to an agent.

Do you have any tips for authors in creating a cohesive theme?

I think filters definitely help make a theme cohesive, but since I don't use one, I can't really make suggestions on this. I think mostly just do what feels right for you. Be authentic and don't try to imitate others. I love seeing cozy feeds with muted color tones, but that's not me. My feed is colorful and chaotic, and even though it might not be magazine worthy, it fits my personality. I think most people know when they stumble across a @xenatine photo, so it works for me—I have a style without using a filter.

I think it's also important as an author to feature books other than your own. Yes, promote yourself, but people also want to see what books you're reading and loving. If you're only posting your own books, it will get boring and repetitive. I would also suggest posting non-book/writing related things in Stories or in Reels instead of on your main feed. Followers like to see your personal life, but if you want to keep your theme cohesive, the best way to do that is to keep your main feed about books and writing.

Chapter 25: BOOK BOXES

Book boxes are a big deal in the bookstagram community. Book box companies usually send out a box a month. These custom printed boxes come with at least one book (usually a hardback new release) and a handful of bookish merchandise that goes along with the theme of the book. The most successful book boxes are focused on Young Adult fantasy and sometimes scifi, but there are romance, middle grade, and thriller boxes. There are boxes for literary fiction and boxes for writers. Customers can buy a single box or subscribe to get one every month.

The books included get a great deal of exposure. Not only are they mailed out to all the customers, but book box companies have a team of Instagramers who get their boxes each month in exchange for posting photos and building interest in the box and the book it features.

Generally, the included books are traditionally published with a lot of buzz around them, but I've seen boxes featuring indie books. They need to be a standalone or first in series, and they are generally from someone with a solid following. Often the company will commission a custom cover to make the book more desirable as a limited edition.

I've also seen book boxes include indie books as a free download with a download card or a print in the box. I've heard mixed reactions on how helpful these are for indie authors. I assume it has a lot to do with how closely your book matches the audience of the box and how good your cover is.

If you're interested in getting your book in a box, follow some book box accounts and get a feel for what sort of stories they tend to include. Email them and ask if they take submissions from authors. These companies are all fairly small businesses and you should usually be able to find someone to talk to. They may also occasionally have a call for submissions. I've included interviews with two boxes that take submissions directly from authors.

You can also put together your own book box! I've seen authors do this for a new release their readers are excited for, or to build buzz for the first in a new series. It's difficult to make a profit with these, but it can be done. It might be better to try and break even and give your fans a special way to connect with your book.

Book boxes could contain:

- A custom printed box

- A custom cover for your book

- Prints of a map or character art

- Bookmarks or stickers featuring your characters

- Treats or hot drinks

- Jewellery that ties into your book

- Custom candles designed for your characters

- Cute socks

- A mug

- A bonus novella

I think this is such a fun idea, and I definitely plan to put one together someday.

INTERVIEW WITH: *Fae Crate*

Owners: Megan and Brittany

Handle: @faecrate for YA fantasy and Sci-fi

@baecrate for adult romance

Website: www.faecrate.com www.baecrate.com

Followers: Fae Crate - 45k Bae Crate - 7.6k

Can you tell me a little about Fae Crate?

Fae Crate first opened all social media pages on January 1st of 2018! It really doesn't feel like it's been that long though. Our box went on sale in February and shipped in March that same year. We both were already established in the book community and Brittany had a shop called @vergeofwisteria that had an established customer base already. From there we grew and our average customer is roughly around 20-30. Our crates focus on Young Adult Fantasy and Science Fiction, so once we choose our book of the month, we build a theme and supporting fandoms around that base. We try to have a mix of reusable items and one time use items so that no matter what kind of merch you like, you will like something inside!

How many boxes do you send out to influencers each month?

We have around 10-15 influencers each month including reps and BookTubers that we send packages to!

How do you choose the books you include? Do you accept submissions?

Yes, we do accept submissions! We have an ongoing release list for 2021, and every time we go to review for a new box, we see which options would do best. We try to include books that show variety each month in diversity. For example, we try to make sure the entire year shows different races, sexualities, etc so that everyone receives a book that they can relate to. It is very important to us to represent as many different storylines as possible since we are all different and have different experiences in life. We do regular calls for self-publishing authors and accept submissions year-round!

You've occasionally worked with indie authors. What is that process like?

We love working with indie authors! In the beginning, we had the setup of including an ebook each month that would be indie or small pub authors. While we were taking books in for these inclusions, we started receiving ARCs of books that were coming out later instead of already out. We decided to look into what it would take to get these created on our own terms! Once we figured out the logistics and tested it out a few times with some amazing authors, we decided to make it a regular thing that is accepted with Fae Crate.

For physical inclusions, books will need to be released within the month and a half before shipping. For regular ebook inclusions each month, the books can already be released! We review these based on the theme for each month and pull titles we have sent to us if we think they would match that theme. If we find a book we'd like to make physical, we will reach out to the author to let them know what all we would need and how we can work together! This process has been so fun for us and really makes us happy as a company to work on these special editions.

If their book is selected for one of your boxes, what can an author do to get the most out of the opportunity?

For ebook inclusions, I would say it is best to share the announcement when we post about it! Some authors have asked if they could host an author takeover on our social media and we love having them. For physical inclusions, we usually offer our authors the chance to host a giveaway for a free Fae Crate the month they're included.

Of course, sharing announcements is important, but we also include a photo challenge in each crate that has our subscribers share photos of their books! Saving these photos on an Instagram album for future use could be awesome to store up promotional material. Honestly, if our authors have any ideas on interaction, we are open to talking about ideas and figuring new things out!

INTERVIEW WITH: *Nerdy Book Box*

Owners: Tamara @nerdybookmama
Handle: @nerdybookbox
Website: www.nerdybookbox.com
Followers: 1.5k

Can you tell me a little about Nerdy Book Box?

Nerdy Book Box is a brand new monthly subscription box service. We were founded at the end of July, and started taking pre-orders for our September boxes in August of 2020. Our customers are book lovers, authors, and other small business owners that want to support our cause and purpose. Each box contains a paperback book (usually with an exclusive cover), and 4-6 products and/or items that are themed to the book. We saw a lot of book box companies curate items that are book inspired or influenced in nature, but rarely did they create a box completely around the book they featured. We wanted to change that.

How many boxes do you send out to customers and influencers each month?

Currently, because we are new and still in the process of growing, we sent out 65 boxes for the month of September. Right now, our active subscriptions are about 60, but because we offer the ability to skip a month, we'll be sending around 50 boxes in October (unless we sell more/out in the next couple of weeks).

How do you choose the books you include?

We have a form on our website that asks pertinent questions to authors, publishers, and other small businesses. We ask for wholesale pricing and shipping information in order to budget accordingly for every month that we curate a box. We are flexible in terms of the age and type of book. We mostly consider: ratings, engagement, aesthetic of the book, flexibility of the author, the ability to get exclusive covers, etc. There are many variables we consider when reviewing books for the boxes. We want to keep things interesting by not including the same genre over and over.

If you choose to work with an author, what is that process like?

When we decide we'd like to feature a book/author in our box (after reviewing our submissions), we will then reach out to the selected author and verify some information on their form. We usually ask to verify pricing, shipping, cost of exclusive covers, what they would want to see included in the box, etc. We want them to be involved in the curation process, because that is something that is important to us.

Once we have decided pricing and items they may want to see, we will purchase books from the author directly. Then we reach out to vendors and get pricing on the items. We become a mediator between the wishes of the author and the shops. When everything is finalized and we come to a mutual agreement, we will order and purchase all said items, have them shipped to us, and put together the boxes. We try and keep the process simple and streamlined in order to keep up efficiency.

If their book is selected for one of your boxes, what can an author do on Instagram to get the most out of the opportunity?

Marketing, marketing, marketing. If the author can mention us to their followers, to their mailing list subscribers, to any and all of their social media platforms, that is how we're able to grow and get more subscribers on board. That is the best way to grow their exposure, as well as expose our company to more audiences.

We have to work together to create hype and interest in the products and goods in the box, but more importantly, to create interest in the indie books. With so much competition in the bookish box world, we wanted to stand out and do something different. That is why we decided to cater to and support indie authors.

Chapter 26: WORKING WITH ARTISTS

A cool thing about Instagram is the various communities and how they intersect. There's a thriving artist community on Instagram, and it's a great place to find someone who can illustrate your next cover, map, or character art. As an illustrator, I use it myself as a way to find clients, and I've hired an artist I found on Instagram to do a character illustration for me.

Here are some things to think about if you're considering hiring an artist through Instagram:

Do they do book-related art already?

There is a huge benefit to working with an artist who does a lot of bookish fanart and has an established following. If they post the art they did for you on their feed, and tag you in their post, you can get a lot of eyes on your story. Artists who draw book fanart will have followers who read and who specifically love the characters the artist draws. Having your characters appear in their feed alongside their favorites is great advertising.

This summer, I hired an artist who is well loved in the book community to draw a romantic illustration of the main characters of my book. When she posted it on her feed, I gained 150 fans and sold 19 books in a 24-hour period, just from her post. While that obviously didn't pay for the art in one day, it was a pretty great bonus.

Do they do the specific sort of work you're interested in?

It's always wise to choose someone who's strong in the kind of art you want. Not just someone who's talented and you can afford. Just because an artist can draw one subject well doesn't necessarily mean they will be able to draw what you want well. And working outside of what they most enjoy drawing will result in work that isn't as good.

Are they consistently awesome?

Do you just love one or two illustrations in their gallery? Half of them? All of them? What if you ended up with a piece as good as the worst thing they've drawn this year? When you hire an artist, you don't know if you'll get their strongest work or not. That can have to do with time, mood, inspiration, and mental health. Sometimes the magic happens, and sometimes it doesn't. Be sure to hire someone that consistently puts out work you're happy with.

What do their past clients say about them?

It's okay to go through their feed, see if they've tagged authors they've worked with, and contact those authors to ask about their experiences. This will help you avoid someone who's flaky or hard to work with.

That's a lot of things, so how do we find these magical creatures?

I'm always paying attention when other authors post art they've commissioned to see what I think. Another great way to find artists is to go through the feed of book boxes who hire a lot of artists (Fairyloot and Faecrate are excellent for this). Their artists tend to have a good-sized following who love books and are also artists who regularly do professional work.

How to contact an artist on Instagram:

You can try sending a Direct Message, but not everyone checks them regularly, especially as messages from strangers are shunted into their "requests" inbox. The best thing to do is find out how to email them. Some artists will have an email button activated on their profile, and most will have a link in their bio to their portfolio website which will include contact information.

Even if you don't hire them, following bookish artists on Instagram can be a lot of fun. I sometimes learn about new books I want to read after being enthralled by a beautiful character illustration, and the art can be a great thing to share in your Stories from time to time.

INTERVIEW WITH: *Arz28*

Handle: @arz28
Followers: 52.1k
Account style: Bookish illustrator
Genre: YA and some Historical Romance

How did you get started doing bookish art?

In my first year of college, my friends and I would bond over Viktoria Ridzel's (@viria94)) artwork on the Percy Jackson series. We adored how she could capture the characters and the scenes from the books perfectly! I was so inspired by her work, but it wasn't until two years later that I tried my hand at digital art. By that time, I was also reading a lot of YA fantasy books, so I posted some fan art on Instagram just for fun. Much to my surprise, the posts started to gain some traction, and through that, I got to meet people who loved the same books as I did.

They've since encouraged me to continue creating artwork based on the books I've read.

What makes an awesome illustration client?

For me, it's always great when the client is clear on what they want from the illustrator and is open to collaborating. It's important to have enough reference on the characters or scene so we can get a good vision and direction on how the artwork will go. Since we do the visual part of the process, sometimes not all the words and details can be translated into one single piece. This is why it's crucial for both the client and illustrator to go back and forth throughout the process to decide what looks best.

What's a mistake authors sometimes make when trying to commission art?

Jumping between different email addresses or not introducing themselves properly. I get a lot of mail from time to time, so I realized I needed to be smart about which projects to take that would fit on a monthly schedule. If you're trying to commission an artwork, please include a subject line or a quick description of the project you're planning to work on, and inform the artist/illustrator about specific deadlines for the commission ahead of time.

What are some ways authors and book boxes have used your art?

I usually do illustrations for pre-order campaigns/promotional work. The same goes for book boxes, but sometimes I get projects from these companies to design custom merch which is always interesting for me.

Any other tips for authors who want to work with an illustrator?

Use a formal-sounding email address. Oftentimes, I check the address listed on the email. I don't mean to judge (haha) but please do not send one as urw0rstnYtmare101@mail.com only to come back a few days later using another email address wondering why you haven't received any response. Just a tip. :)

Take the time to learn about artist/illustrator rates. It varies from one project to another, so talk with the artist beforehand until you come up with an agreement.

Give honest feedback. Every artist/illustrator has a different creative process, but it is important for us to know your thoughts on each update to see if there are changes needed before the final artwork is sent.

Final Thoughts

TROUBLESHOOTING

Have you been plugging away at Instagram for a while and just not seeing growth? Here are some things to check:

Have you been doing it for long enough?

Growth can be slow, especially if you don't have a large fan base for your books yet. It might take a year or more to break 1k followers. If you want to grow your Instagram following, it's going to take perseverance.

Are your images good enough?

You don't need to be a professional photographer, but clear, well-lit photos are going to get you more followers.

Be honest, is your phone's camera cutting it? Maybe ask a friend what they think.

Are you posting things people are interested in?

I get a lot more engagement on very popular books, so I pick a few that I honestly like in my genre and sprinkle them amongst my other posts. Remember, your account is designed to engage readers of your books and books like yours.

Are you starting each caption with a question?

I honestly can't stress this enough!

Are you using hashtags and changing them often?

And above all, are you interacting in the community?

You need to get out there and comment on other people's posts. Share their feeds in your Stories. Be a good community member and it will come back around to you.

CONCLUSION

Thanks for nerding out with me about Instagram! I hope you're feeling inspired to go forth and grow your platform. Remember, don't try and do all of this at once. Just pick a couple things that inspire you and have fun with them.

A giant thank you to all the people who took the time to share their knowledge with us in this book. I learned a ton from them, and I hope you did too! If you skipped the interviews, you might want to go back and read them. My advice may not suit your personality and genre, but

I've included a range of authors and influencers to help you figure out what will work best for your account.

At the back of the book, I've included some resources for you, including all the apps and websites mentioned in the main book and the interviews. There's also a list of all the accounts interviewed, and a glossary of slang and terms that might help if you're new to Instagram. These resources can also be found on my website:

www.InstagramForFictionAuthors.com.

Good luck!

@HannaSandvig

RESOURCES

Photo Editing Apps

A Color Story: https://acolorstory.com

Snapseed: https://snapseed.online

Pixaloop (animations): https://www.pixaloopapp.com

Photoshop Express: https://www.adobe.com/ca/products/photoshop-express.html

Lightroom (mobile): https://helpx.adobe.com/lightroom-cc/how-to/lightroom-mobile.html

Instasize (make borders): https://instasize.com

VSCO: https://vsco.co

Photo Lab: https://photolab.me

Werble (animations): https://www.werbleapp.com

Snow: https://snow.me

Planning Apps

Later: https://later.com

Planoly: https://www.planoly.com

Hootsuite: https://hootsuite.com

Computer Programs

Lightroom Classic: https://www.adobe.com/ca/products/photoshop-lightroom-classic.html

Photoshop: https://www.adobe.com/ca/products/photoshop.html

Bookstagram Challenges

Bookstagram Challenge Organizer: https://kelljasmer.com/challenges

Challenges of Bookstagram: https://www.instagram.com/challengesofbookstagram

Bookstagram Challenges: https://www.instagram.com/bookstagramchallenges

Link Services

Linktree: https://linktr.ee

Url.bio: https://url.bio

Hashtag Finders

IQ Hashtags: https://iqhashtags.com

All Hashtags: https://www.all-hashtag.com

Ingramer: https://ingramer.com

For Display Purposes Only: https://displaypurposes.com

Banned Hashtags: https://app.iqhashtags.com/en/banned-hashtags-checker

Other Websites

Bookbrush (3D mockups): https://bookbrush.com

Canva (graphics): https://www.canva.com

Cherry Pie Author Services (bookstagram style photography): msha.ke/cherrypieauthorservices

Book Tour Services:

Storygram Tours: http://www.storygramtours.com

Book of Matches Media: https://www.instagram.com/bookofmatchesmedia

MTMC: https://mtmctours.com

Instagram Courses

Alana Albertson: www.authoralanaalbertson.com

Sarah Moore: https://newleaf-writing.teachable.com/p/Instagram-and-bookstagram

ACCOUNTS INTERVIEWED

Authors

@hannasandvig

@authoralanaalbertson

@kimwritesbooks

@authorcarolinegeorge

@kealanpatrick

@chelscey

@thesenovelthoughts

@danielleljensen

@jamesfahyauthor

@becky_moynihan

@_ckarys

@_mkarys

@kandisteiner

@kaylmoody

@tyffany.h

@valialind

@brianamorganbooks

@author_j.m.buckler

@audreygreyauthor

Influencers

@read.write.coffee

@newleafwriter

@everlasting.charm

@darkfaerietales_

@myfriendsarefiction

@xenatine

@nerdybookmama

@theguywiththebook

Other

@storygramtours

@storygramkids

@faecrate

@baecrate

@nerdybookbox

@arz28

GLOSSARY

Book Haul - the books you bought that month

Bookish - book related

Booksta - bookstagram

Comment Pods - a group who comments on each other's posts

DM - **D**irect **M**essage

Engagement Groups - a group that likes and/or saves each other's posts

Feed - all your photos. Confusingly, can also be all the photos you are shown

Filters - an editing effect you apply to a photo

Flat lay - a photo taken from directly above objects on a flat surface.

IGTV - Instagram **TV** (similar to YouTube)

Insta - Instagram (also IG)

Live - live streaming video

Merch - merchandise

OTP - **O**ne **T**rue **P**airing (your favorite fictional couple)

Reels - short videos (usually with music)

Rep - representative (someone who helps promote a brand in return for free product)

Ship - characters you want to have a romantic relationship (you ship them)

Stories - short videos and images that disappear after 24 hours (similar to Snapchat)

Street Team - readers who help you promote your book

TBR - **T**o **B**e **R**ead (you can have a TBR for the month, a TBR stack, a TBR shelf, and you can add something to your TBR)

Theme - the overall look of your feed

Unboxing - a video or photo of opening something you bought or were sent to promote

Wrap-up - the books you read that month

ACKNOWLEDGEMENTS

Thanks to everyone who answered my interview questions! This book was a group effort, which is so representative of Instagram and the amazing bookish community there.

A huge thank you to my beta readers, Kirstin, Clari, Kim, Heather, Elizabeth, Alison, Tessonja, and Rose. This book is so much stronger with your help, not to mention more accurate. Thank you to my mom, Valerie, for your edits, and to my editor, Becky, for once again fixing all my commas. Thanks to my typo hunters, Karen and Christine.

Thank you to God, for all your good gifts to me, including this amazing online community and the friends I've made there.

.

Made in the USA
Coppell, TX
12 December 2020